Larrikin Days

For Robert from all of us at
Nicholson Street School.

Thank you for visiting us.

Rosa Pickard
22. 2. 1991

Front endpaper: Mort Bay, Balmain (1979)
Back endpaper: Peacock Point, Balmain (1979)

Larrikin Days

100 YEARS OF GROWING UP IN AN AUSTRALIAN SUBURB

Tony Stephens with Annette O'Neill

Nicholson Street Public School
Parents & Citizens Association
in association with John Ferguson, Sydney

Waterview (now Mort) Bay, 1870 *(NSW Government Printer)*

Authors' Note

The authors wish to thank all those who offered words and photographs. There were too many to list individually, but special acknowledgment is made to the Mitchell Library, the Hall and the Hardin families, Barry Thomas, John Wright, Marjorie Wane, Jennie Bates, Peter Reynolds, Harry Leo, Bob Lundie, Lillian Robyns and Jean Schofield.

First Published in 1983 by
Nicholson Street Public School
Parents & Citizens Association
Nicholson Street
Balmain NSW 2041

In association with
John Ferguson Pty Ltd
133 Macquarie Street
Sydney NSW 2000

Designed and produced by
John Ferguson Pty Ltd

ISBN 0 9591988 0 6

994.4′1

Printed in Australia by Macarthur Press Pty Ltd

Larrikin Days was published with the help of a grant from the New South Wales Government's Division of Cultural Activities

Contents

LARRIKIN: noun. Colloquial

1. (formerly) a rough and sometimes violent young man.
2. young person who gets up to tricks.

Balmain from Observatory Hill, 1882 *(NSW Archives)*

Balmain from Observatory Hill, 1982

Introduction

I'm h-a-p-p-y
I'm h-a-p-p-y
I know I am, I'm sure I am
I'm h-a-p-p-y.

Neville Wran, Premier of New South Wales, remembers singing those words at Nicholson Street School, Balmain, in the early 1930s. They were Depression days and not everyone was "h-a-p-p-y". It cannot be easy for a child to wear a smile on his face when there is not enough food in his belly nor, on cold winter mornings, shoes for his feet.

"I was probably the only kid in the school who had a pair of shoes," Wran said in 1982. "Not probably, I was." These were black days for Balmain, black days in towns and suburbs across Australia, black days for the whole western world. Western democracies were engaged in the first of their two great struggles of the last 50 years, the struggle for the survival of industrial capitalism. The second great struggle, the war against fascism, was just a few years off.

In this less-than-satisfactory world, Australian schoolchildren were ordered to sing of their happiness. As if happiness can be ordered. At Nicholson Street, if the child's heart were not in the song, teacher Miss Gertude Goulding would rap him or her over the knuckles with, as Wran put it "a bloody great stick".

Children still sing "I'm h-a-p-p-y" at some schools today, usually during a class on religion. They sang in the 1930s under the influence of Christian bourgeois imperialism. They sing in the 1980s under no particular influence at all or, perhaps, under a multitude of confusing influences. They sing now in the age of uncertainty.

Yet the adults and the teachers, the parents and the preachers, got it wrong. They need not have ordered the kids to chorus their happiness; for the young have always been good at finding happiness. It is true that adult memories of childhood are coloured by defence mechanisms which shut out the pain of the past. It is also true that, as their parents struggled through the black days of the 1930s, the children of Nicholson Street thought their days were golden.

In that less-than-satisfactory world, Nicholson Street often seemed the best of all possible worlds. They were fun days. Making boats from sheets of tin stolen from the Adelaide Steamship Company in Mort Bay and rowing across to Goat Island or Balls Head; diving off the back of ferries bound for Erskine Street in the city; fishing and prawning, catching crabs and scraping mussels; catching the tram up Darling Street to see the "flicks" at the Amusu; riding the tram "dummy" down to Darling Street wharf; stealing fruit from neighbours' trees; sailing with the men on the 18–footers. Golden days.

Balmain is, at one and the same time, a microcosm of Australian suburbs and something a little apart — a village within a city. The idea for this book grew out of plans to celebrate the centenary in 1983 of Nicholson Street School. It is not a history of a school; nor a history of a suburb. It is an attempt to paint — with old photographs and the memories of people who lived there — social sketches of an Australian suburb through 100 years to 1983, with the school as a focal point.

It remains essentially a book about Balmain. But it is also a book about Australia growing up. Many of the sketches will be familiar to the people of Carlton or Collingwood, for example. All Australians were affected by the glorification in the schools of the ideals of the Empire, by the harshness of the Depression, by the grim reality of the war effort.

The book, then, will appeal to the nostalgic. It will also have relevance today in a nation that has fallen again upon hard times. The young today find it difficult to cope with hard times. Politicians and economists and teachers have rammed progress down their throats. They have been told that, with reasonable hard work, a little good luck, and lots of good weather, life in Australia would get even better, inexorably and inevitably. In 1983, that is nonsense. It has been nonsense for most of the last hundred years. Count the years through adult eyes: there have been about 60 years in which the country has been blighted by war, depression, recession, bust or general grimness, and 40 good years in which Australia has experienced peace and prosperity. Golden days 40, Black days 60. Children don't score it that way.

1882 map of Balmain

1

"How about you call me John and I'll call you Prince?"

FROM BOILERMAKER TO PREMIER

Balmain has always had a lot to do with boats. Residents used to build them and muck about in them. They based industries on boats, they fought in and over boats. They made love in boats — or used boats to travel from home to a harbour island or a secluded harbour foreshore where they could make love in peace and quiet.

William John Storey sailed from Sunderland, County Durham, in the 1860s to become a pioneer shipbuilder of Australia, bringing his wife, Elizabeth Ann, and two children. They settled on the south coast of New South Wales and had four more children while Mr Storey built ships at Jervis Bay and Bateman's Bay. Storey thought the future of the shipbuilding industry was in Sydney, but didn't live to see it eventuate. The A.L.P. official journal, the *Standard Weekly* recorded in 1944, that Mrs Storey had packed her children in an open boat, sailed from the Clyde River to Bateman's Bay, and then on to Balmain. Early accounts suggest the boat was 24 ft (7 m) long; later descriptions put it at 16 ft (5 m). Whatever the size of the vessel, it was a voyage of considerable courage.

John Storey, one of the children on board, was aged six when his mother's little boat nudged alongside the Balmain peninsula. He was educated at Adolphus Street School. This was a Church of England denominational school, attached to Saint Mary's, East Balmain, until the Public Instruction Act of 1880. In 1882, the church leased the Adolphus Street schoolroom to the Department of Public Instruction until the Nicholson Street building was ready. John C. Waterman, later principal at Nicholson Street, was Storey's first master at Adolphus Street.

Storey served seven years apprenticeship as a boilermaker with the firm of Perdriau and West, as the *Sun,* 5 October 1921 records, thus forging a link between Balmain boilermaking and political leadership — Sir William McKell was a Balmain boilermaker; so, too, was Sir John Kerr's father. When he became a journeyman, Storey worked at Mort's Dock. Explosions in boilers were not uncommon those days, killing several Balmain wage earners. The young Storey started campaigning for a Land Boilers Inspection Bill. "If I was in Parliament," he told his mates, "I'd soon show them!" He won the seat of Balmain in 1901.

John Storey was included in the government formed by William Holman in 1913. When Holman resigned in 1916 because his Labour Party conference wanted the abolition of the Legislative Council, Storey took up the reins of power and quoted *Macbeth:*

To be thus is nothing;
But to be safely thus.

Holman went away and worked out a compromise with his party, returning as leader within 24 hours. Storey wasn't too disappointed: although his election had been a personal triumph, it was at the expense of party solidarity. "It is something to have greatness thrust upon you," he said, "if only for half a day."

Storey fought Holman and Billy Hughes, a citizen of Balmain identified with the conscription issue. Those, like Storey, who opposed conscription were sometimes called unpatriotic. Storey declared: "I believe in peace by negotiation. So do my three sons in the trenches. If all the men and women who *talked* patriotism had their families boiled down, there would not be a decent family amongst them", quoted a political reporter in the *Sun* 23 June 1918. Dr H. V. Evatt, who later won the Balmain seat for Labor, said: "Storey became an astute debater and a very vigorous and very direct speaker". He was known as "Honest John" Storey, an admirable epithet for a politician.

He had played first grade cricket for Balmain, loved horseracing, and was of a genial, homely breed. And when he was elected Premier of New South Wales in March 1920, the family recorded that this song was written, with apologies to *Gilbert and Sullivan:*

When I was a nipper I made my name
Rivetting bolts on a boiler frame.
At rivetting bolts I learned some tricks,
So I rivetted my mind on politics.
And I rivetted my mind so skilfully
That now I'm the Honourable John Storey.
Chorus: *And he rivetted his mind so skilfully,*
That now he is the Honourable John Storey.

The Prince of Wales (later known as the Duke of Windsor) visited Australia that year. Storey's daughter-in-law, who wrote about his meeting with His Royal Highness, reported that the Honourable John Storey began: "I'm not quite sure how to address you, so would you mind calling me John, and I'll call you prince". The Prince persuaded the Premier to take an impromptu train journey to Newcastle, lending the unprepared Premier a pair of royal pyjamas.

But Storey was dead soon after, in October 1921, from Bright's disease and heart disease. He hadn't had much time to translate a State Premier's authority into legislation, although he had sponsored measures to increase the basic wage and had sold state bread over shop counters in competition with private industry. The *Sydney Morning Herald* thought him acceptable because he was a good deal less radical than some of his colleagues. And the people of New South Wales mourned sincerely, with the funeral procession measuring a mile and a half long. Among the family mourners was John Storey junior, who later became chairman and managing director of Repco and then director of aircraft production during World War II. He approved the construction of the Beaufort, a torpedo bomber, and the Beaufighter, and travelled with Prime Minister Robert Menzies to Britain. Menzies had this member of a distinguished family — son of a Labor Premier, grandson of a Balmain boatbuilder — knighted.

What was Balmain like when the Storey family went there in the 1870s?

William Balmain had arrived in 1788 on Captain Arthur Phillip's First Fleet to Australia, where he began service as Second Assistant Surgeon. He fought a duel with Principal Surgeon John White, both participants being only slightly wounded; such were the rigours of life in the colony. For most of the time Balmain worked hard, set up Sydney's first tent hospital, lived with a convict girl, Margaret Dawson, and became Principal Surgeon.

The early governors of the colony rewarded civil and military personnel with grants of land and Governor John Hunter so rewarded William Balmain in 1800 — with 550 acres of what is now Balmain and Rozelle. But Hunter stated that the land be known as Gilchrist Place and Balmain transferred the land title in 1801 — for 5s — to John Borthwick Gilchrist, a Scottish surgeon serving in Calcutta, India. The story of the grant is one of the recurrent mysteries of early Australian history. The most likely explanation is that Balmain owed Gilchrist money for a shipment of goods, including alcoholic spirits, from India. The 1801 sale is immortalised in a once-common Sydney saying: "It's all Balmain to five bob".

Early settlers first used Balmain as a picnic place. Visitors landed from boats on the rocky shore and what were sandy beaches. Kangaroo hunts were staged with the animals being driven all the way from present-day Leichhardt and Ashfield down to Peacock Point or Long Nose Point.

Captain Hugh Morwick, an old sea captain told how in 1838, at the age of 16, he had landed at Peacock Point from his English sailing ship, collected oysters from the rocks and climbed the ridge to what is now Nicholson Street. Captain McLean, Superintendent of Convicts, settled at Peacock Point. The cows, from his dairy farm, ambling to and from their pastures at Leichhardt, made the track which is now Darling Street. Branch roads sprang from Darling Street down to the water on either side of the peninsula. The social ascendancy phase of Balmain's development grew from the 1830s to the 1850s, when the Gilchrist grant was broken up. Substantial houses were built with lofty ceilings, cedar stairs and doors, wide verandahs, servants' quarters and spacious gardens. Sea captains, especially, found it a desirable place to live. Captain John Nicholson built Durham Hall, in Nicholson Street, went bankrupt in the 1841 depression and leased it for use as the Captain Cook Hotel. Thomas Robert Allt, wine and spirit merchant, lived there when it was restored as a house. Modest houses of stone, timber and brick were built. Ferry services began from wharves dotted around the peninsula.

Shipbuilding and associated industries brought the next — the industrial — phase. Timber merchants and chemical manufacturers followed. Captain Thomas Stevenson Rowntree bought land for a dock, began building in 1854, and was joined by Thomas Sutcliffe Mort, who preferred to live in the less smoky confines of Greenoaks, now Bishopscourt, Darling Point. Workers moved in to live near their jobs and by 1881, the population was 15 063. The affluent were starting to move out, although quite ornate terraces were built for the middle classes. Nothing was planned, however. Soap was manufactured at White Bay from 1895 and the Sydney Colliery Enabling Act of

1897 cleared the way for the sinking of coal mine shafts next to Birchgrove School. The writing was on the wall for Balmain as a pleasant living environment. The trend was not to be reversed until the 1960s.

They were larrikin days. Frederick Ward, known as Captain Thunderbolt the bushranger, escaped from the jail on Cockatoo Island. He swam across the harbour, disregarding the sharks, and disappeared into the Balmain bush. He was shot dead in 1870. Ned Kelly was hanged in 1881.

They were boom days, too. Belief in progress had not been diminished by the survival of barbarism in the bush. Men and women believed they had acquired three things with which to establish their dominion over the continent — the railway, the telegraph and education. Not more than half the children of parents other than those in the government, public service, military, banking or landowning establishment had attended school in 1860. In 1880 Sir Henry Parkes introduced the bill which became the Public Instruction Act, severing the ties between church and state and establishing the basic framework for education in New South Wales. Waifs who had wandered the streets on weekdays disappeared from sight. Within a decade of the introduction of compulsory education there were complaints that the ignorant larrikins who prowled the streets at night and at weekends were being replaced by educated larrikins.

Parkes, who lived in Hampton Villa, East Balmain for a time, wrote: "It alone [education] has the power to awaken the humbler classes to a true sense of the dignity of humanity, and inspire them with a true love of equality and order combined, which is the true foundation of freedom". Roman Catholic Archbishop Vaughan took a different view, describing the national schools as "the seed-plots of future immorality, infidelity and lawlessness". Parkes won the battle, if not the war. His 1880 Act, proclaiming "free, compulsory and secular" education, withdrew state aid from the denominational schools. It took over 80 years and a Menzies government to reintroduce it and there was fire again in 1983 debates over state aid to private schools.

Nicholson Street was among many schools that continued to charge fees, attendance remained voluntary for years and learning was touched with Protestantism. In May 1884, Nicholson Street Principal, Peter Wallace wrote to W.J. Trickett, Minister for Public Instruction, about the need for a Work Mistress. The average attendance of girls was over 70 — out of the 159 enrolled in infants and primary departments. The enrolment of boys was recorded as 221 making a total of 380 pupils. There are about 120 enrolled today.

In August 1884, Henry Allen, an unemployed shipwright of Cooper Street, wrote to the Minister:

> I have over seven children in my family and I find it very hard to meet expenses my children attend school regularly I hope you will kindly excuse the payment of the above account. I have the honer [sic] to be Sir your obedient servant. . .

The letter carried no punctuation and the amount of the account was not stated, but records show that Allen still owed 6s 9d in May 1888.

Nicholson Street School was designed in a formal style by William Edmund Kemp, had five classrooms and cost £5300, plus £2029 18s 11d for the land. Leaders of the community of Balmain — with the exception of the Catholic Church — welcomed the school's establishment, while wondering about the future of the growing school population as the suburb changed from being rich and fashionable to poor and industrial. This trend particularly worried "the best type of Balmain womanhood", the principal members of the Balmain Benevolent Society: Mrs Hannah Broomfield, Mrs Bracegirdle, Mrs Macdougall, Mrs Maides, Mrs Parker, Mrs Morwick, Mrs Carruthers and Mrs Law.

A meeting of the Balmain Benevolent Society in 1886 decided that a study of eugenics — methods of improving the quality of the human race, especially by selective breeding — be encouraged. Mr S.N. Hogg, a bank manager and the society's honorary treasurer, wrote:

> To visit the sick, to comfort the distressed, to give food to hungry children is indeed good, but we are convinced that brains as well as big hearts are needed if the evil is to be grappled with as it should be. The root causes of poverty strike deep. Nevertheless, and until eradicated, the Balmain Benevolent Society strives hard to remove their surface evidences — to cleanse the festering sores and soothe them with the ointment of charity. . .
>
> By the insufficient control of drink traffic, by tolerating slum-lords, and, perhaps most of all, by the criminal neglect of the laws of eugenics, we are breeding poverty, for Benevolent Societies do but trim and lop the branches which our legislators allow to grow crooked and ugly.

The larrikins of Balmain were, if this benevolent society had its way, to be weeded out.

Balmain about 1875 looking down Darling Street to East End

Steam Ferry Bay, 1870s (now Jubilee Bay)

Mort Bay, 1883, taken from the bottom of Nicholson Street

Nicholson Street class in 1880s. The first school photo extant *(Wane Collection, Balmain Association)*

Nicholson Street, early years. Louisa Killeen second left, front row

Reconstruction of a class of the 1880s *(NSW Department of Education)*

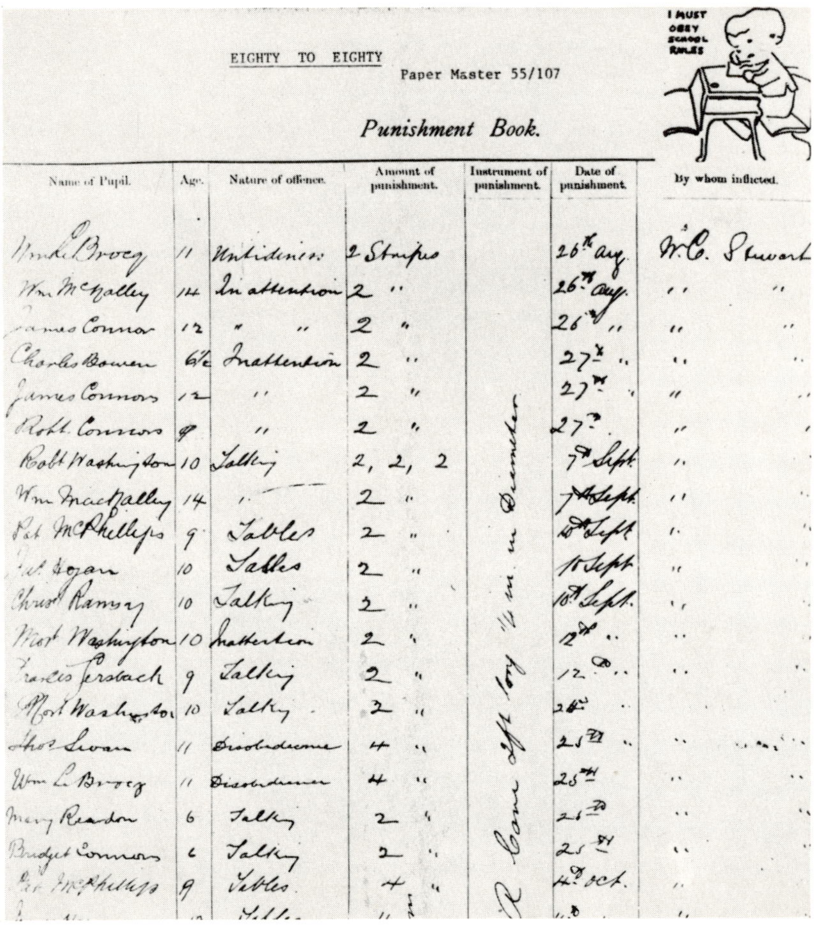

EIGHTY TO EIGHTY

Paper Master 55/107

Punishment Book.

Name of Pupil.	Age.	Nature of offence.	Amount of punishment.	Instrument of punishment.	Date of punishment.	By whom inflicted.
Wm L. Brocq	11	Untidiness	2 Stripes		26th Aug.	W. C. Stewart
Wm McNalley	14	Inattention	2 "		26th Aug.	" "
James Connor	12	" "	2 "		26th "	" "
Charles Bowen	6½	Inattention	2 "		27th "	" "
James Connors	12	"	2 "		27th "	" "
Robt. Connors	9	"	2 "		27th	" "
Robt Washington	10	Talking	2, 2, 2		7th Sept.	" "
Wm MacNalley	14	"	2 "		7th Sept.	" "
Pat McPhillips	9	Tables	2 "		10th Sept.	" "
Pat. Hogan	10	Tables	2 "		10 Sept.	" "
Chrisr Ramsay	10	Talking	2 "		18th Sept.	" "
Mort Washington	10	Inattention	2 "		2nd ..	" "
Frances Jersbach	9	Talking	2 "		12th ..	" "
Mort Washington	10	Talking	2 "		24th ..	" "
Thos Sivan	11	Disobedience	4 "		25th ..	" "
Wm L. Brocq	11	Disobedience	4 "		25th	" "
Mary Reardon	6	Talking	2 "		25th	" "
Bridget Connors	6	Talking	2 "		25th	" "
Pat McPhillips	9	Tables	4 "		4th Oct.	" "
[illegible]	[illegible]	Tables	[illegible]		[illegible]	"

(Written vertically in the Instrument of punishment column: R Came left Sydney ½ m. in December)

Punishment book

John Storey

Premier John Storey meets the Prince of Wales, later the Duke of Windsor

John Storey's funeral cortege moves up George Street
(photos on this page from the Storey family)

Sunday, a Melanesian, with Sheila Tucker

Nicholson Street class photo, about 1910

2

"A white man, though black of skin"

BALMAIN IN THE 1880s

One pupil at Nicholson Street School in the 1880s was called Sunday. His real name was Malatau, but he was a black boy and the white people of Balmain, of British and Irish stock, found the name Malatau decidedly foreign. The black boy first met a white man on a Sunday. If Robinson Crusoe could have a Man Friday, Balmain could have a Sunday. So Sunday he became.

The circumstances of the meeting were extraordinary, according to subsequent newspaper reports and descriptions passed down through the family that adopted him. Captain John Dickie Harley was a master mariner from Scotland who encountered Malatau in the New Hebrides about 1870, when the boy was three years old. A Sydney newspaper, reporting Sunday's death 45 years later, wrote:

> The Island of Santa Cruz was then full of cannibals, and the little child was just ready for roasting when Captain Harley came upon the scent [sic] and the good-natured "salt" bartered to buy and save the child's life. He succeeded and brought the baby on to Sydney, but when Mrs Harley saw it she told her husband to take it away again with him, jocularly reminding him that he had previously brought home a monkey, which had let down all the newly washed clothes from off the line, on a wet day at that. The Captain took the boy away, but kept him on his vessel, and brought him back again, when Mrs Harley took pity on him and brought him up.
>
> From the danger of the cannibals' fire, Sunday became quite an identity of Balmain East. He was educated at the Public School by Mr J.C. Waterman, and for 45 years has resided in this suburb. He was for years a regular attendant at the Campbell Street Presbyterian Sunday school and church, under the late Dr Cosh, and he became an earnest Christian, in fact, an example to many professing white Christians. He was well-known and respected in the neighbourhood in which he lived, and the children were always friendly to Sunday. . . He passed away in the same quiet manner in which he lived.

The practice of bringing Melanesians into Balmain was not uncommon. Mrs Sheila Goldsmith, 82 years old in 1983, remembered Sunday with affection. Mrs Goldsmith was born Sheila Tucker in Hosking Street, now a site for town houses but then looking over a sandy beach. Boys and girls would get up early to play on the beach and splash about in the water before going to school.

Sheila's brother Holden drowned there one horrible day. The beach was never the same after that. But Sunday helped ease the pain, taking her gently on his knee. Mrs Goldsmith later said of him:

> Grandfather bought Sunday for a string of beads. I worshipped him. When I was about five I said to him, "Sunday your face is black". And he said, "Oh, I must have a wash". We didn't know his birthday so we would give him a party on New Year's Day. He used to "first foot" us — if the first man over the threshhold on New Year's Day was dark, you were lucky. Sunday would come in with a bottle in one hand and a cake in the other. He was a happy soul, making money by picking up bottles, doing odd jobs round the house and following the 18–footer races. If he had a winning bet on a boat he would give us a penny chocolate.

The New Year of 1883 had opened full of promise. Queen Victoria was still on her throne and God in his heaven. A man named L'Estrange was optimistic enough to try to walk across Sydney harbour — by means of a cable, but a spoilsport put an end to that idea by cutting the cable. The *Sydney Mail* of 13 January carried news dated 1 December 1882, from London via Suez, on the P & O steamship *Clyde,* then overland from Melbourne. The newspaper also carried "intercolonial" news from Brisbane and Melbourne. Australian cricketers were engaged on their home grounds in a battle for the Ashes against the Hon. Ivo Bligh's tourists and two Australians — W.L. Murdoch and F.R. "the Demon" Spofforth — came from Balmain. The Czar of Russia ordered a "Te Deum" sung in the Winter Palace and proposed the health of the Emperor of Germany.

The rateable value of land in Sydney was £1 691 895, meetings discussed extending the railway line from Redfern to Circular Quay, and "The Sketcher" wrote in the *Sydney Mail* of 27 January 1883: "One of these days, before the end of the world, there may be a bridge across from Sydney, and in the greater hereafter that exquisitely beautiful piece of territory [North Sydney] may be inhabited and enjoyed by others besides a few daring market gardeners".

"The Sketcher" also wrote:

> Balmain came in spite of almost everything adapted to drive the most inveterate settler from it. Wind, ill odours, difficulties of access, and what not, utterly failed to prevent a few desperate spirits from cleaving to its rocks, like oysters. St Leonards, always more pretentious, with simply incomparable advantages. . .

Larrikinism was rampant, the *Sydney Mail* recorded.

> Larrikinism grows and spreads — intrudes its noxious presence in all places alike; everyone asks what is to be done, or suggests the use of the "cat", the establishment of reformatories or of industrial schools; and only a few suggest (and they are counted fools for their pains) that it might be as well to try to teach children to know and to do the right, rather than to wait till they have done wrong, and then either convert or transport them.

Youths were continually before Balmain courts for objectionable behaviour in the streets and it was a phenomenon that was not going to fade away. Mr H. Austin, of Balmain, complained to a newspaper in 1899 about larrikins in local parks, calling the youths "the scum of the town". He advised that the parks should be closed and wondered how tenants could be found for homes in the area.

The ladies of Sydney seemed oblivious to the larrikins. They wore net and lace to Government House parties, silks and satins, puffs and frills, tight-fitting basque bodices and bonnets. A sign of the growing use of the electric light was the popularity of a colour called "electric blue" at the most fashionable gatherings. The ladies were having such a lovely time, it seems, that they were sleeping in rather too often. "Phyllis" of the *Sydney Mail* advised her readers that such slothful behaviour would lead to "pale faces, unhealthy constitutions, feeble characters and diseased lungs" and pervert their "whole being, physical and moral, from the healthy type". In conclusion "Phyllis" urged: "The girls here are doubtless very attractive, but they might add much to their charms if they would turn out of their beds a little earlier".

Balmain held its own balls. According to S.N. Hogg, they were "delightful balls, attended by the elite of Sydney". Hogg wrote: "Balmain was decidedly the fashionable suburb in those days, and particularly so at the East End". On these occasions the young women had attentions "bestowed on them by young naval officers from the warships — British and foreign — in dock at Balmain, whose presence at their fathers' homes in uniform lent distinction to the ballroom".

Captain John Broomfield, who lived at Glentworth, opposite Saint Mary's, was a sea captain who entertained in his ballroom, billiard room or exotic garden overlooking Johnston Bay. His neighbours at one time or another included Thomas Robert Allt, James Peter Franki of Mort's Dock, Canon Stack and the Captains Rowntree, Banks, Lyons, Trouton, Bracegirdle, Harrold, Braithwaite, Fletcher, Napier, Morwick, McClements and Sustenance. They helped Balmain have a last fling as a fashionable society.

Owen S. Evans was the best-known Balmain doctor of that time. He lived next to Saint Mary's, visited homes on horseback or in an old-fashioned gig, entered through the kitchen door rather than lose time at the front door, and was a man of few words to patients. S.N. Hogg reported that in 1889,

> Dr. Evans was driving a restive horse about whose perverse disposition he had been warned to be careful; the animal shied at some object in the road and the gig, of which the doctor was the sole occupant, collided with the pavement at a spot opposite the Congregational Church.

The doctor died when his head struck the kerbing.

There was a certain amount of violence in the classroom, too. James Walton, of Peacock Point, complained to the Secretary of the Board of Education that his daughter, Edith, had been beaten brutally on the arms and back of the neck with a cane and made to stand with her face to the wall for two hours over "some trifling fault". Peter Wallace, the principal, said Edith, aged 12, had been persistently disobedient and he had removed her from the class, gently remonstrated with her and "touched her very slightly once with the cane". The department chided Wallace for not using forbearance, said the involvement of teacher Fanny Drewe was "reprehensible", and lifted Edith Walton's suspension. After eight-year-old Marian Meeklah was given three cuts of the cane for having five mistakes in dictation, the department's Inspector R.N. Morris warned that caning for mistakes was not approved, but teachers were authorised to give corporal punishment in moderation for serious breaches of discipline.

Other people had other problems. Captain George Corkhill, of Nicholson Street, asked the Under Secretary for Public Instruction in 1886 for permission to "make use of a part of the schoolground for the purpose of playing Lawn Tennis occasionally (after school hours, of course)". The department refused permission. However the department cancelled a debt of Henry Allen, who owed £1 5s in school fees though blaming, in part, intemperance; the man himself had said he was "very poor" and as for bread there was "nowhere to get a lofe [*sic*]".

Lists of parents owing fees reflect the onset of economic recession from 1886. The women often took in laundry; most of the men were unemployed shipwrights, sailors or labourers; and alcohol was a problem. Hard times at home might also have brought a certain rebelliousness in the schools — the authority of the teacher was challenged in a way the Victorian Age had not seen before.

The 1880s had begun with a boom. The inhibitions of the Victorian Age were breaking down. The University of Sydney accepted its first enrolments of women in 1881, the year after the *Bulletin,* to become a home for some of the best Australian writers and critics, was first published. Primary industry was booming, on the backs of the sheep. Industrial Balmain was booming, attracting workers. And building societies were coming into their own, lending to homebuilders for their brick terraces and timber cottages.

"Balmain is a working men's suburb," the *Balmain Observer* reported in 1885, "and anything which will tend to improve their position should always be welcomed". The writer announced the floating of a building society, the Balmain Investment, Land and Building Company, with a capital of £500 000.

But by 1890, the British had withdrawn investments, largely because of the failure of speculative investments in the Argentine, and the banks were in trouble. Building societies collapsed. There were major strikes in the transport, coal mining and wool industries. William Lane, Mary Gilmore and others despairingly planned to leave Australia and create a "pure socialism" in Paraquay.

It was in 1890 that William Morris "Billy" Hughes came to Balmain. A man of small stature, he proceeded to set up a mixed business in 16 Beattie Street with his wife, eventually became Prime Minister of Australia, and presided over the conscription fight during World War I. Hughes lost the fight to have conscription introduced. Three great political events have traumatised the Australian Labor Party since its formation: the first was conscription. The second was the conflict between communists and right-wingers in the 1950s that led to the emergence of the Democratic Labor Party and cost Dr H.V. Evatt any chance he had of leading the country. The third occurred in 1975, when Governor-General Sir John Kerr sacked the elected government of Prime Minister Gough Whitlam. Balmain identities have been at the centre of all three traumas.

Balmain was formative for Hughes; from his Beattie Street shop he sold second-hand books, mended locks and repaired umbrellas – and he spoke to the people on Saturday nights on the corner of Beattie and Darling Streets, near the pub, Unity Hall. Andrew Stevens, of Balmain, recalled in the 1950s how he carried Hughes's "spruiking box and lamp" there. In front of Hughes as he spoke was Loyalty Square. The World War I monument, bearing the words "liberty", "peace", "honour", and "empire" was to be built close to the speaker's place of address. As Donald Horne has pointed out, those were key words in the Hughes rhetoric. After lecturing the locals on Saturday nights, Hughes lectured Sydney at large on Sundays, taking his box to The Domain.

The miners' strike of 1890 lasted two months and tens of thousands of workers in other industries lost their jobs. The unions lost the battle in these strikes but they led to the formation of the first Labor Electoral League — in Balmain. Hughes was in the New South Wales Parliament in 1894 and in federal politics in 1901. Expelled from the ALP in 1916, he helped form the Nationalist Party. He was expelled from the Nationalists in 1929, tried to form his own Australia Party and joined the United Australia Party. Expelled from the United Australia Party in 1944, he joined the Menzies Liberal Party in 1945. Asked why he had never joined the Country (National) Party, the former Balmain radical said: "You have to draw the line somewhere".

Advertisement from the *Sydney Mail,* 1883

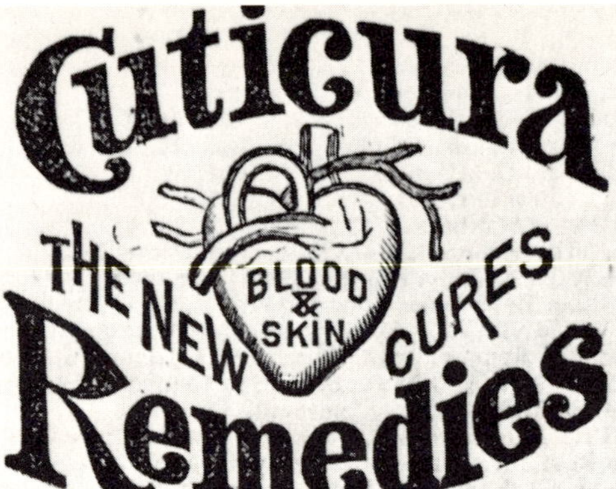

Scald Head. Eczema.

Cuticura Resolvent, the new blood purifier internally, and **Cuticura** and **Cuticura Soap,** the great skin cures externally, clear the Complexion, cleanse the Skin and Scalp and purify the Blood of every species of Itching, Scaly, Pimply, Scrofulous, Mercurial and Cancerous Humours, Sores, Ulcers, Swellings, Tumours, Abscesses, Blood Poisons, Scurvy, Salt Rheum, Erysipelas, and all other Torturing Disfigurations, Skin Blemishes and Humours of Childhood, when physicians, hospitals, and all other means fail.

Scrofula on Neck.

Cuticura Resolvent operates with energy upon the bowels, liver, kidneys, and pores of the skin, purifying the system of all humours and diseases arising from impure blood, inherited weaknesses, and mercurial poisons.

Cuticura, a medicinal jelly, clears off all external evidence of blood, skin, and scalp homours, eats away dead skin and flesh, instantly allays itchings and irritations, softens, soothes, and heals. Worth its weight in gold for any itching humour, itching piles, and delicate irritations.

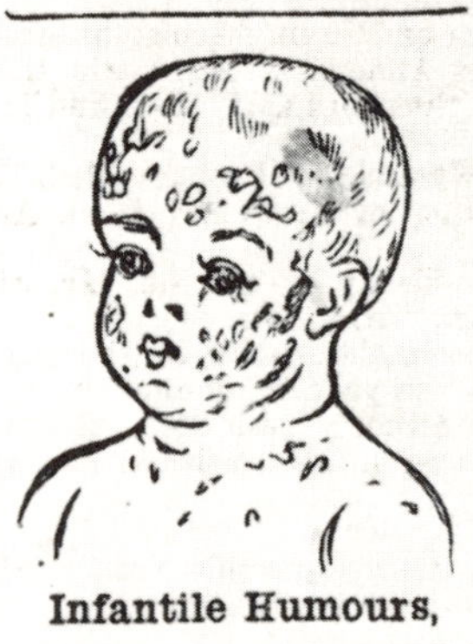

Infantile Humours,

Cuticura Soap, fragrant with delicious flower odours and healing balsams, contains in a modified form all the virtues of Cuticura, and is indispensable in treating skin diseases, and for restoring, preserving, and beautifying the complexion and skin. Indorsed by physicians and chemists as the purest Baby Soap. The Cuticura Remedies are the only real curatives for diseases of the skin, scalp, and blood, and may be used from infancy to old age. Price, Cuticura Resolvent, 4s 6d per bottle; Cuticura, 2s 9d per box; large boxes, 4s 6d. Cuticura Medicinal Toilet Soap, 1s 1½d; Cuticura Medicinal Shaving Soap, 9d. Sold by all dealers. Prepared by WEEKS and POTTER, Boston, U. S. A. R. TOWNS and CO., Sydney, Consignees,

☞ A 64-page medical work, illustrated with coloured plates drawn from actual cases cured by Cuticura Remedies, mailed on receipt of two 3-cent stamps.

"FOR THE BLOOD IS THE LIFE."

CLARKE'S

WORLD-FAMED

BLOOD MIXTURE

For CLEANSING and CLEARING the BLOOD from all impurities, cannot be too highly recommended.

For Scrofula, Scurvy, Skin diseases, and Sores of all kinds, it is a never-failing and permanent cure

It Cures Old Sores
Cures Ulcerated Sores on the Neck
Cures Ulcerated Sore Legs
Cures Blackheads or Pimples on the Face
Cures Cancerous Ulcers
Cures Blood and Skin Diseases
Cures Glandular Swellings
Clears the Blood from all Impure Matter
From whatever cause arising.

As this Mixture is pleasant to the taste and warranted free from anything injurious to the most delicate constitution of either sex, the proprietors solicit sufferers to give it a trial to test its value.

THOUSANDS OF TESTIMONIALS FROM ALL PARTS.

Sold in bottles 2s 6d each, and in cases, containing six times the quantity, 11s each—sufficient to effect a permanent cure in the great majority of long-standing cases—by all CHEMISTS and PATENT MEDICINE VENDORS throughout the world. Proprietors, "The Lincoln and Midland Counties' Drug Company," Lincoln, England.

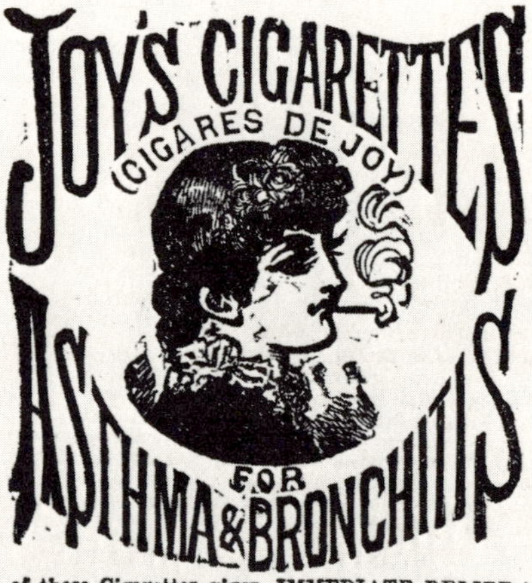

One of these Cigarettes gives IMMEDIATE RELIEF in the worst attack of ASTHMA, HAY FEVER, CHRONIC BRONCHITIS, INFLUENZA, COUGH, and SHORTNESS OF BREATH, and their daily use effects a COMPLETE CURE. The contraction of the air tubes, which causes tightness of chest and difficulty of breathing, is at once lessened by inhaling the medicated smoke of the Cigarette; a free expectoration ensues, and the breathing organs resume their natural action. Persons who suffer at night with COUGHING, PHLEGM, and SHORT BREATH find them invaluable, as they instantly check the spasm, promote sleep, and allow the patient to pass a good night.

These Cigarettes have been successfully tested and recommended by the Medical Professi on for many years. They are perfectly harmless, and can be smoked by ladies, children, and the most delicate patients, as they are pleasant to use and contain no substance capable of deranging the system.

Agents in Australia: FELTON, GRIMWADE, & Co., Melbourne; ELLIOTT BROTHERS, Sydney; ELLIOTT BROTHERS & Co., Brisbane; FAULDING & Co., Adelaide. In New Zealand: KEMPTHORNE, PROSSER & Co., Dunedin, Auckland, Christchurch, and Wellington. NONE GENUINE UNLESS SIGNED ON BOX "E. W. WILCOX."

Advertisements from the *Sydney Mail,* 1883

Old house in Balmain, 1906

Jubilee Dock, 1890s. Photo taken by Francis Killeen

Sunday school teachers at St Marys, 1893

Congregational Church, Darling Street and Curtis Road, about 1900

3

"A bosun's whistle for a mother's call"

SAILING INTO THE TWENTIETH CENTURY

In 1983 Wee Georgie Robinson was restoring a yacht to put in Sydney's Maritime Museum. The yacht, the 18-footer *Britannia,* was built by Robinson in six weeks way back in 1919, fastening her with 7200 copper nails, every one of them dipped in varnish before being driven into the cedar. They don't make boats like the *Britannia* today. They don't make many men like Georgie, either.

Robinson was to turn 90 in August 1983. He was at Nicholson Street School in Federation year, 1901. His father, Jacky Robinson, was a blacksmith and brought the family — there were seven children — from Pyrmont to Balmain when Georgie was five. Robinson senior worked from 6 am to 6 pm at Pyrmont, rowing to and from his home every day. He sailed a 22-footer at weekends in the 1890s. The stake for match races sometimes reached £100 a side — in days when £200 represented two years' wages for the working men in the crews. His father died at 93 years of age. "He would have made 100," said Georgie, "but he fell off a jetty and broke a hip."

Miss Gertrude Goulding took up a post as a temporary teacher at Nicholson Street in 1901. She didn't leave Balmain, for retirement, until 1936, having taught more children of the suburb than anyone else in the last hundred years. Georgie remembers her fondly even if Neville Wran doesn't share his attachment — Miss Goulding had been teaching Nicholson Street kids for 30 years by the time Wran went to school and the years may have wearied her. Robinson recalls that the school teacher rubbed sandsoap on the tongues of boys she had heard swearing. He didn't like school much but he never wagged it. "If you did, you landed on the *Sobraon.*" The *Sobraon* was a clipper ship moored off Cockatoo Island and used as a training school for wayward boys. She had succeeded the *Vernon* in 1890, the latter vessel having been bought expressly for this purpose after Sir Henry Parkes became concerned about the numbers of homeless, illiterate boys roaming the streets. The youngest boy on the *Vernon* in 1883 was aged only five, hearing "a bos'n's whistle for a mother's call".

Robinson became an apprentice boatbuilder, built his own six-footer in 1914 and then the *Britannia.* The history of the growth of Australia to nationhood can be told through the achievements of its sporting heroes. Wee Georgie played a part in that growth.

When England first played an Australian team at cricket, the leaders of the empire allowed the inferior colonials 22 men against the English XI. Subsequently there were Australian 18s and Australian 15s. The nation reacted with considerable joy when an

Australian XI ultimately played an English XI, a joy matched as much by the first victory of an Australian XI as by such events as the Federation of Australian states. The achievements of Australian rowers were greeted with similar national acclaim. Ted Trickett, born on the shores of the Parramatta River, became the first Australian to be recognised as a world sporting champion by beating English champion J.H. Sadler in a match race on the Thames in 1876. Australians won 32 out of 45 contests for the world professional sculling title between that year and 1914. William Beach carried the black and gold colours of Balmain to victory.

For this part, Wee Georgie helped to democratise sailing. The Balmain sailors wanted no part of the convention-bound, genteel way of nineteenth-century yachting. They were wharflabourers, shipwrights, miners, labourers and factory hands. They played football in the winter and sailed in the summer. The *Britannia* carried up to 3000 sq ft (279 sq m) of sail and up to 14 crew, most of them in black and gold football jerseys. They helped bring egalitarianism to sport.

Wee Georgie played first grade Rugby League for Balmain in 1915, weighing just 7 st 11 lb (49 kg) and measuring 4 ft 11½ in (151 cm) tall. He played for New South Wales against New Zealand and England and coached Balmain's President Cup teams for 38 years from 1915. At after-school cricket he once batted for a week in Pilcher's Paddock, now the White Bay container terminal. Arthur Mailey, the Balmain captain and Australian bowler, complimented Wee Georgie about his sporting talent in this way: "You're a better cricketer than a footballer".

After school he used to row over to the city under Observatory Hill and across to Pyrmont Bridge, collecting beer bottles bobbing about the harbour and selling them for a penny a bottle. "There were chooks, too," said Robinson, "sitting up on the piers under the wharves. Somehow they'd got out of the ships that had brought them down from north coast farms. If you were quick enough, you had a nice dinner."

Georgie's son Ron, also a boatbuilder, was in Neville Wran's class. "I learned Neville how to row a boat and swim," said Georgie. He gave Neville a rabbit one day. And the young Wran would help hang up the *Britannia's* sails to dry.

Robinson remembers the Balmain Colliery disaster of 1900. The shafts extended eastward to the main workings; 64 acres (26 ha) under Ball's Head, Goat Island and the entrance to Mort Bay. There had been plans to lay the shafts from the north side of the harbour but the citizens of those suburbs had been more vocal in their opposition. The mine was never economically viable and was closed in 1931, but not before several fatal accidents occurred, including the deaths of five men in 1900. Six men got into a bucket to descend the shaft, then 1770 ft (540 m) deep. At about 1400 ft (427 m), the bucket tipped over, throwing five of the men 300 ft (91 m) down the shaft. "To give, if possible, a darker shade to the tragedy, one of the bodies fell at the feet of a brother who was working below, and a second at the feet of his own father", the *Balmain Observer* reported.

There is little evidence that Australians were moved by the spirit of nationalism in 1901. They had other matters on their minds: the Boer War, bubonic plague and the death, on January 23, of Queen Victoria. She passed away soon after patting her favourite

Pomeranian dog, leaving the empire on which the sun never set in the hands of the less virtuous Edward VII. John Norton, editor of *Truth,* had been acquitted of sedition by a Sydney jury in 1896 after having asked God to save the Queen, indeed "to keep her rascal of a turf-swindling, card-sharping, wife-debauching, boozing, rowdy of a son, Albert Edward, Prince of Wales, off the throne". The people of the King's Balmain no doubt sympathised with Edward's larrikin streak, but wondered if it were appropriate to a new monarch.

Balmain Council had decided on special measures to end the plague, which reached Sydney in 1900. Houses were to be inspected closely, all rubbish was to be burned, and the council would make a large purchase of poison for the rats. "Only yesterday a large number of rats were seen fighting for a bit of bread at the corner of Johnston Street," the council was warned.

And the people wondered about the standard of education their children were receiving. Asked by inspectors to explain poor school results, principal Jason Graham pointed in September 1901, to epidemics of influenza, measles and scarlet fever and the fact that four teachers at Nicholson Street had been ill. Former principal Waterman had blamed, in part, the weather. But the poor results were to continue for years, despite the blandishments of certain education authorities.

None of this bothered little Thelma Duff. Thelma's sister Vera had been at Nicholson Street for several years by the time the younger girl enrolled on her seventh birthday in 1908. In 1983 she recalled her first day at school:

> I was nervous. I had waited for this day and Vera took me down to Miss Goulding and she sent Vera away and she put her arm round me and she said, "Don't be frightened dear, I'm going to sit you right close to me and, when I'm free, I will help you". They are her very words. I will never forget. I loved her and I just looked on her as another mother. She put her arm around me and she just sat me there near her desk and I was as right as rain. I trusted her, you see.

Thelma Duff was to have a career on the stage. One of her first performances was for those wayward boys on the *Sobraon.* "I was only four or five . . . it was before I went to school. I remember I did the cakewalk, a little prancing dance that was fashionable in those days, and a duet with my partner, Marie McLaughlin". Marie went to St Augustine's Roman Catholic school opposite Balmain Public School, known as the Pigeon Ground because men once shot pigeons there for sport. The priest sent for Marie one day because he had a complaint about one of the children singing a bad song in a show they were giving:

There was I, waiting at the church
Waiting at the church, waiting at the church.
Can't get away, to marry you today.
My wife, won't let me.

That was considered naughty in those days. But the priest asked her to sing it right through and he said: "All right, I don't think there's anything wrong with that". And sent her away.

One of Thelma's grandfathers was a British sea captain, a grandmother was a schoolteacher in England, her father was in charge of Dalgety's imports division, and an uncle owned several substantial hotels around Sydney. "I shouldn't say it but I think we looked down our noses a bit at most of the other people in Balmain. We weren't encouraged to mix. We were told to be polite, to say, 'How do you do?', but we were never allowed to go into people's places and they didn't come into ours". Balmain has never been quite as egalitarian a place as its supporters claim. It is true that there has usually been a broader range of socio-economic groups in Balmain than in other Australian suburbs, from the time the sea captains were joined by the boilermakers, to today, when the lawyers, academics and business executives share the territory with the artisans and labourers who were the essence of Balmain for the first six decades of the twentieth century. They share the territory; but they don't share much time together.

Thelma and Vera, and their brothers Leslie and William, were read a page of the Bible and a page of Shakespeare every day at home. Thelma says:

> Everybody loved my father. Every Saturday night he'd say, "Come, my girl" and I'd link his arm, just like an old lady, and we used to walk up Darling Street for Saturday night shopping. We would talk to people in the shops and father would say later, "There my girl, are people who are born Christians". When he died we were in mourning for six months. My uncle locked his daughter's piano for six months and I even had a little grey dress with black.

The family moved to Randwick. Thelma remembers her mother saying: "When all's said and done, it's a better suburb. If you live among prosperous people, you'll feel more prosperous".

The *Balmain Observer,* however, had welcomed the idea that Balmain was fast becoming an industrial suburb, adding that the suburb would be, one day, "the Birmingham of the mother state of the great Commonwealth".

Building blocks costing £2 deposit and £1 a month were being advertised; Nicholson Street baths offered "the cleanest and best baths in or near Sydney", with a sandy beach. About this time other public baths — a floating wooden enclosure — were built at the bottom of Johnston Street; Alexander Johnson was charged with driving a motor car faster than a walk in Darling Street; there was relief over the fact that gambling Chinese had been driven out of the district, and concern among drinkers that police had cracked down on pubs that opened illegally on Sundays.

The first public kerosene lamp had been installed near Darling Street wharf, primarily as a beacon for boatmen who used the white sandy beach there. The lamp, as Reginald Thornton and A.W. Sommerville, authors of *Balmain Retrospect* note, also served as a safety guide for drinkers falling out of the nearby Shipwrights' Arms late at night. Electric street lighting was switched on in 1909, Thornton and Sommerville record, although most families still relied on ice chests to keep food cool — buying a large cube of ice from the visiting iceman every second day — or even a meat safe hanging in a cool place and covered with wet canvas.

Health measures were tightened after the plague. For a nation concerned that it would be overrun by the Russians, the Chinese or the Japanese, the fall in the birth rate from 38 per thousand people in 1870 to 27 per thousand people in 1900, encouraged governments to concentrate more on the health of the babies that were born. Contraceptives were called "race suicide" and banned from advertising; the 1903 report of the New South Wales inquiry into the birth rate was destroyed as an obscene publication. There is little evidence one way or another but the chances are that Balmain men and women, with a fair percentage of Irish Catholics and a fair ignorance of available contraceptive methods, did their bit for the country. They had large families, with ten and more children being quite common.

Balmain's connection to the sewerage system brought problems as well as relief. Captain Frederick Bracegirdle, who had a flag pole in his front garden and a son as aide-de-camp to a Governor of New South Wales, complained in 1907 that rock left from excavation work provided the boys in Balmain with "plenty of ammunition to throw at the locusts, not caring on whose head the stone may drop". In 1910, 242 pupils were enrolled at the Nicholson Street School but Senior Inspector M. Beavis said: "It is open to question whether the school should ever have been established where it is. Perhaps its continuance is involved in the question of accommodation to be provided for Balmain Superior Public School. [The Pigeon Ground School at Gladstone Park]". By April 1912, enrolments at Nicholson Street were back to 379, with Gertrude Goulding taking up to 67 in her 1A class.

Mrs Georgina Willson was Miss Georgina Elphinstone when she knew the Miss Goulding of the pre-World War I years: "She had a lovely cup and saucer and the kids used to love to wash it up". She remembers the Irish and the Scots dominating the East End of Balmain. The area was fairly happily integrated, although there was some bigotry between churches, the Labor Party was thought by some to be dominated by Catholics, and green was an undesirable colour to some people. Rough porridge, boiled rice with sugar and nutmeg were staple foods — and fresh, crusty bread with a twist on top.

There are more Robinsons in Balmain than there are Smiths. Billo is not related to Wee Georgia or to Latchem. But he is the brother of Junka, who died aged 88 years in 1981. Billo, Junka, and six other children lived with their mother in a tiny stone house opposite the Balmain Bowling Club. Someone always had to sleep on the floor. Billo doesn't remember his father, a sailor who just sailed away one day. His mother spoke six or seven languages and talked of having lived in Gibraltar but she remained a mystery too.

Billo, who was an altar boy in the church, began school at Saint Augustine's and used to take the school's cow to and from Pilcher's Paddock to graze. His mother later thought too much religion might weaken his mind so she packed him off to Nicholson Street. He said in 1983:

> I used to take a bag to school and, on the way home, fill it with washing from houses in Darling Street. I'd deliver it to the laundry, then return it. We couldn't afford anything. I used to go to school without boots. Then I won a competition — a bursary — which would have got me to any school — but I had to go out to work. We used to have a competition at school every Friday — girls versus the

boys — testing your knowledge. You'd get sixpence if you won. I won pretty often. I topped the class. They called me "The Dux".

Junka wasn't such a successful student. His brother regretfully stated:

The only school he went to was Brush Farm, the reform school. He did two years there. He came home and, within half an hour, he'd pinched again. He jumped over a counter — the ham and beef shop — and took the bloody till and all. When he got pinched a second time he came up before the magistrate who said "blah, blah, blah" and sentenced him to another two years. Me mother gets up and says, "Your honour, could you make it three?" He said, "If that's the way you want it, ma'am, yes". So he went up there for three bloody years.

Free again, Junka quickly established himself as one of the best sportsmen around. He played Rugby League for New South Wales and was chosen for an Australian team that toured New Zealand.

After leaving school, Billo delivered newspapers on horseback and eventually became a tug and lighter skipper. He recalled the diet of bread and dripping for breakfast and toast and dripping for tea, the evening meal called dinner by some residents in Balmain: "You'd hold the fork with the bread in front of the fire and burn your bloody fingers. But you didn't seem to get crook. There weren't too many weaklings around".

There was a certain rebelliousness about the Robinsons, like many Balmain families. Billo was a bit young for World War I. However, for all males between 12 and 25 there was compulsory training. As the lights went out over the world, Billo was locked up for refusing to drill properly.

Butcher shop now laundromat

H. COPESTAKE

Wholesale, Retail and Family Butcher

Contractor to New South Wales Government.

...197 & 199 DARLING STREET...

Telephone: 62 Balmain.

The Oldest Established Butcher in Balmain.

Working Men's Institute, about 1900 *(Balmain Association)*

Bootmaker, Darling Street Rozelle, 1911

Boys drill on the *Sobraon*

Below decks on the *Sobraon*

Looking down Stephen Street to the old ferry wharf

Boys from the *Sobraon* march up Cove Street

Balmain Fire Station, 1904

Mort's Dock 1905

Pay day at Mort's Dock, about 1904

The 18 footer *Britannia*

Balmain sailors picnic, Middle Harbour 1918. Wee Georgie Robinson is fifth from the right in the second front row, while Tony Russell, with hat peeps between two other hats at rear

Two Balmain heroes: Junka Robinson *(left)* and Chook Fraser at Birchgrove Oval, at the end of World War I

The Balmain sailors took their girls to their picnic at Middle Harbour in 1919. Wee Georgie is third from right in the second front row

A class of 1912

Stan Robinson, captain of the soccer team in 1916

1st and 2nd class, probably 1914. Jack Morgan fourth from left in back row and Bob Lundie far right in same row

Nicholson Street fete for war victims, 1915

4

"We set off in a shower of flowers"

WORLD WAR I

The monuments remain. In country towns across Australia they often stand in the middle of the main street, the names carved into the stone to serve forever as silent policemen of the passing traffic. If the main street is on a hill, the monument commands the heights of the town, only questioned by the church spires and challenging that the dead not be forgotten. Few nations can have made such a public display of their dead.

Monuments are less obvious in the city suburbs. Most have been pushed to the roadside; others are in the church or have been taken inside the RSL Club, along with the poker machines. The most obvious war monument in Balmain divides the traffic in Darling Street near Beattie Street, the spot where Billy "The Little Digger" Hughes used to address the dissatisfied workers from his soapbox. It used to be known as Loyalty Square, but few people call it by that name these days. Most taxi drivers have never heard of Loyalty Square. They know the Unity Hall Hotel, though, and Woolworths over the road, and the Balmain Tiger dry cleaners.

The monument bears the words "peace", "honour", "empire" and "liberty", and 38 names are carved into its now flaking sandstone. There are 113 names on the honour roll at Saint Mary's and 123 on the roll at the Campbell Street Presbyterian Church, plus 64 from the Rozelle Church of England honour roll, brought to Balmain when the two parishes were amalgamated. Of 255 men who enlisted from Saint John's, Birchgrove, 57 were killed. Not to mention the Methodists, the Roman Catholics, the Congregationalists and even the odd atheist, who went to the war to end all wars. Halfway throught the war the *Balmain Observer* ran an incomplete honours list of people who had enlisted. It carried 506 names.

It is impossible to tell exactly how many Balmain people went to that war and how many people did not come back. The War Memorial in Canberra doesn't know. The Central Army Records office in Melbourne doesn't know. The RSL doesn't know. They all know the grand totals: 59 342 Australians were killed and 166 817 wounded, extraordinary figures considering the country's population was about five million.

Consider those figures, look at the honour rolls and a picture of the nation's commitment to war emerges. There were just over 32 000 people in Balmain before war broke out and only about 5 000 men of that suburb old enough, but not too old, to serve. In the brief, previously mentioned history entitled *Balmain Retrospect* written in 1935, Thornton and Sommerville wrote: "Although it is impossible to obtain a complete record of the number of enlistments from Balmain, it is known that nearly all of the eligible young men saw active service on land and on sea, and of these, many made the Supreme Sacrifice''. The sacrificial ones have crowns against their names on the honour rolls — or crosses.

The schools had produced the cannon fodder. Patrick J. Nelligen, a headmaster in Balmain, said as much:

> The crowning glory of the schools is in the record of the thousands who have passed through their portals and have proved worthy citizens, with the aspirations of an enlightened democracy. The response of the great call of Empire when the Balmain youth joined his fellow Australians in the desperate struggle proved how effective had been the teaching and influence of the schools, in inculcating love of country, freedom and justice.

God, it seemed, was on both sides. Lowther Clarke, the Anglican Archbishop of Melbourne, preached on the Sunday after war was declared that it was God's plan, even if it did make that commandment about loving one's enemy a bit difficult to fulfil. This contradiction of the times was reported in the *Freeman's Journal,* 14 August 1914. A young German wrote later: ''We had set off in a shower of flowers, intoxicated by roses and blood. For the war must bring us what was great, powerful and solemn. To us it wore the aspect of a cheerful shooting match on flowery meadows bedewed with blood''. For young people brought up on the inevitability of progress, the carnage of the Great War must have come as a terrible shock.

The honour roll at Saint Mary's was presented by Mr J.P. Franki, managing director of Mort's Dock and Engineering Co., and Mrs Franki, ''In loving memory of Lance Corporal Stirling Napier Franki'' (their son), killed at Pozieres in 1916. William Edward Mazey, aged 20, had died at the same place a few days previously. Randolph Edward Edge was one of several who fell at Gallipoli. Five Howell Prices are mentioned on the roll of enlistments, three Seamans and several families sent two young men.

Bill Dutton, who later taught at Nicholson Street, was boarding in Leichhardt as a schoolboy at the time of the war, and he said of the phenomenon:

> The two sons of the family with whom I was staying went off to Gallipoli together. One went missing there and was never heard of again. The second survived, then went to France, where he fought until the end of the war. Then came Armistice. The parents were delighted. But they got news that the second son had died in the very last days of the war. What a terrible thing.

Colour Sergeant Patrick Killeen came from Ireland to Balmain in the 1830s with the 17th Regiment. He settled with his wife, Honoria, on Johnston's Bay, in the street which now bears their name. His grandchildren, Louisa and Francis, were at Nicholson Street during the nineteenth century. Louisa's world was cultured, yet insular. She was courted by her nextdoor neighbour, George Wane, whose family also belonged to the Saint Mary's Church of England congregation across the road. George was an avid sailor of his 18-footer, an accomplished flautist and an amateur photographer. The Wanes and the Killeens were part of a group not very common in Balmain around the turn of the century, in that they came neither from the ranks of the prosperous sea captains nor from the labouring classes, but were somewhere in between.

George and Louisa's children, Doreen and Marjorie, attended Nicholson Street before and during the war and Doreen went on to become principal of Sydney Girl's High School. Uncle Francis, who volunteered in the family tradition and lost a leg at Gallipoli, became first president of the Limbless Soldiers' Association.

Mortimer Hugh Froude went to school at the Pigeon Ground, to church at Saint John's, and was the first boy to join the newly formed Royal Australian Navy. Froude was confirmed into his church just two weeks before joining the Navy. Three days later war was declared. The 15-year-old was soon sailing to the war zone on the flagship, HMAS *Australia.* He was transferred to the Royal Navy vessel, HMS *Defence* and his last letter home was written ten days before the Battle of Jutland. He died in that battle, along with 11 500 other British and German sailors.

George Munroe Porter was quick off the mark, too. His sister, Madeleine Porter, aged 89, said in 1983:

> He was on duty outside a barracks — in some sort of civilian capacity. Someone shouted the war was on and he dashed in to sign up. He was No. 803 in the war. The first 802 must have been awfully quick. My mother was amazed. I couldn't understand it either. He sailed for New Guinea on the *Berrima,* the first Navy ship out of Sydney Harbour. But, the night before she sailed, she was moored off Cockatoo Island and we could see the troops on the deck. I'll never forget that.

Another brother, Sid Porter, went to France. He wrote poems about his experiences which have been published and broadcast. One is about the death of a mate, Alfred Waterfield, in a dugout they shared on the western front, at Merricourt:

And the bitter truth dawned on me
when I lifted up his head,
that his ashen face was lifeless
and I knew that he was dead.
Then my thoughts went to his people,
in our homeland far away.
And I sensed the bitter anguish
of their tragic loss that day.

Henry Lawson and Banjo Paterson used to go to the Morgan home in Darling Street, sometimes to read or write, sometimes to talk and drink. Young Jack Morgan, who later became the East End chemist, recalled Lawson in sandshoes and an old suit. Morgan's father, John Stanton Morgan, came back from the Boer War a captain. "My father was a dreadful drunk but a gifted journalist," said his son. "He told me, 'In wars, there are no heroes — only blokes who want to get away from their wives or blokes who are broke'." John Stanton Morgan died in France in 1918.

In 1983, Jack Morgan remembered Armistice Day: "All the big Balmain ferries were taking 200 and 300 people into Sydney to celebrate. There was hardly anyone left in Balmain. It was one of those rare occasions".

Not everybody responded so enthusiastically to the war or its end. A meeting of the Australian Miners' Association at Broken Hill at the outset of the war resolved: "That this meeting views with sorrow and regret the armed hostilities between the nations of Europe, and we regard the present war as a display of civilized savagery and reversion to barbarism engineered by the financial interests of Europe to suit their own ends". Frederick Burgess, of Balmain, was brought before the court and charged with a breach of discipline on a drill parade.

Magistrate: What do you work at?
Burgess, grinning and playing with his straw hat: I'm doing nothing.
Magistrate: But what do you do when you are working?
Burgess: Oh, anythink [sic].
Laughter
Magistrate: What does your father do?
Burgess: Works in the city.
Magistrate: Yes, but what does he do?
Burgess: He works.
Laughter
Magistrate: Yes, my boy; but what does he work at?
Burgess: Well, at his own business.
Laughter
Magistrate: Yes, but what does he work at? What is his business?
Burgess: Making white ants.
Shrieks of laughter
Solicitor: I suppose you mean he makes stuff to kill white ants.
Burgess: Yes, that's right. Something like that.

Schools held concerts to raise funds for the war effort. Boys and girls knitted socks and other items of clothing to go to the front. Displays of empire loyalty became a regular part of the school week.

All of this meant that the blood flowing abroad tended to overshadow the real reforms made in education in the first decade and a half of the twentieth century. Francis Anderson, Professor of Philosophy at Sydney University, had stirred things up by pointing out at a teachers' meeting that education was neither free nor compulsory, that classes were hopelessly over-enrolled, that teaching methods were mechanical, and that the pupil-teacher system — whereby senior pupils first helped teachers and then went on to teach themselves — was a system that produced poorly educated and inadequately trained teachers. The criticism was taken up in parliament, senior education officials made overseas visits and reforms were introduced basically bringing education closer to real life and emphasising in learning the discovery of information instead of committing facts to memory. A physical example of these reforms came at Nicholson Street in 1911, with the removal of the gallery from which monitors watched the pupils.

John William Benton recommended that the reforms did not go far enough. He concluded one reason the Germans had acquitted themselves so well at war was because of a superior education system. He wanted to experiment with new education systems and wanted the experiments to be carried out in Balmain.

The war was, indeed, a crisis for Benton, but not the first he had faced. He had written to the authorities as long ago as 1888, from a school at Lower Lawrence, near Grafton, a four-mile horseride from his home: "Since I brought my wife here in January 1887, events have been one continuous catastrophe that has culminated in the loss of our infant son, which can be attributed in no slight degree to the wretched accommodation that can be obtained here — a house without fireplace or kitchen".

Benton, up against the barbaric bush, had also drawn the wrath of a father whose daughter had been expelled for not providing the required explanation for not wearing boots. For all that is said about families being too poor to have shoes in "the old days", the fact is that most children preferred bare feet, at least in summer. The authorities also pointed out to Benton that children were less likely to catch colds going barefooted than if they arrived at school in wet boots.

The Grafton floods of 1887 could not have helped. Benton took a steamer to Sydney, worked at various schools and arrived at Nicholson Street in 1916. He came to Balmain on the understanding that he would be allowed to try certain new educational methods formed after years of study and a tour of education institutions in Britain and on the Continent. He submitted to the Education Department that he had invented a phonic alphabet "that provides a new departure point". Benton theorised:

> The course should develop a knowledge that Life is dependent on Laws; that the preparation for this Art of Living which we term Education, is to learn how to search for, discover and formulate laws and to practise obedience to those discovered . . . It may not be uninteresting to recall that it was about a century ago when Prussia, stricken in war, determined on a system of education that has enabled it not merely to regain her footing but to become a most efficient and aggressive nation. While deploring the iniquity of the deeds of aggression, the force and efficiency of the methods must be acknowledged. Prussianism can be conquered and controlled only by our adoption of a sounder, truer, more reasonable and more scientific attitude to life.

On a more practical level, Benton wanted to introduce such subjects as agriculture, gardening, carpentry, leather sewing, elementary surveying, photography and milk and cream testing. He argued that knowledge of nature could be best obtained through working with nature rather than through verbal instruction. He welcomed the pledge by Director of Education, Peter Board, for a "wider scope for free initiative and spontaneous action in the pupil". And he said he had had a "view of a more extensive promised land and much more delightful vital conditions than perhaps Moses ever enjoyed".

This early twentieth-century heretic won considerable support for his causes. A senior departmental officer wrote: "I regard him as having few superiors either in the study of professional literature or power of independent thought on educational problems''.

Benton wanted ''to produce explorers and inventors rather than spongers and imitators''. He said: ''The child should be taught to live rather than to moralize, to act rather than to pose, to be, rather than to seem''.

Phonetic spelling might have been his Achilles heel. He was ordered to discontinue it. The world was not ready for phonetic spelling in 1917 and still wasn't ready in 1983. Benton's visions of reform seemed to collapse around him. Mrs Benton died, then he had a nervous breakdown and retired. John Benton walked out of Nicholson Street for the last time as the lights were about to come back on all over the world. And as Peverley Hall limped back from the war with a wooden leg, to the house almost opposite the school. War had changed him forever.

Louisa and Frank Killeen

Francis Patrick Killeen

George and Henry Wane in the backyard of their home in Darling Street (George has the pipe)

George and Louisa Wane with Dot and Fanny Savage on a picnic, about 1900

The Killeens and the Wanes

Marjorie and Alan Wane. Alan died two weeks after the photo was taken in a fall from a swing

Dorothy and Marjorie Wane, 1917

Bath time, a photo by John Pemberton *(Macleay Museum)*

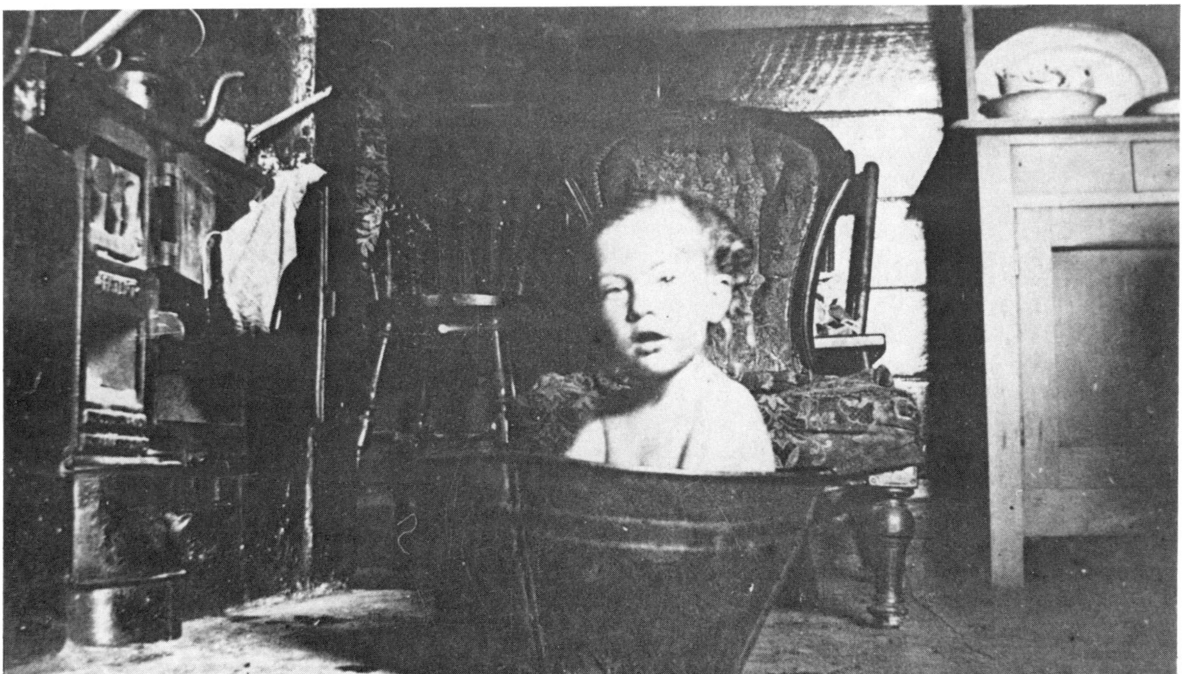

Maypole dance World War I. Eileen Ballerum is in the back row, second from the right

Maypole dance 1983

NSW schoolchildren growing vegetables as part of the war effort, 1917 *(NSW Department of Education)*

Knitters at Nicholson Street, for the war effort

Basketball team, 1919. Eileen Ballerum, Jess Morgan, Edna McKenzie, Myra Glenn and Eileen Schofield are in the front and Jean Schofield, Stella Ballerum, Edie Houster and Olive Baulkwell are at the back

Flag drill for Empire Day, 1919

5

"Jazz crazed people rushed the church"

THE ROARING TWENTIES

Families who had a man coming home from World War I would put out flags and signs saying "Welcome home" or "He's back". The sign hanging almost the length of the upstairs balcony railings at Durham House was white with red letters — in the words of Barbara Foy, author of *Kid Sister,* "a big, proud piece of bunting telling the world".

Arthur John Peverley Hall flew one of those terribly fragile and vulnerable early fighter aircraft and was shot down over Egypt when only 19. The pilot wasn't found for three days, by which time gangrene had taken hold of one leg. The Halls put out their bunting after Armistice Day. The children of Nicholson Street would gape at it with admiration every day. "Isn't your brother coming home *yet*?" It was a year before young Hall, now old beyond his years and his weight reduced from 11 st (70 kg) to 6 st (38 kg), was fit enough to come home. The bunting was dirty and ragged. The Hall children — there were nine others — dressed in their Sunday best of white muslin or blue serge and their father, usually so disciplined about extravagance, took a taxi for the family to meet the ship.

His mother, Suzy Emma Nancy, wrote sentimentally about her son:

> When I get sad and perhaps inclined to think with sorrow of how this accident affected his life, I have only to recall that wonderful shining face of his thro' which the very soul of a conquering hero shone, as he came to greet me, to know that thro' that mighty struggle he had gained eternity, and a thankfulness which brings tears to my eyes bathes me in its healing mist.

His sister Barbara, then an eight-year-old pupil at Nicholson Street, wrote later:

> John with a wooden leg; a dreadful, heavy contraption with a big leather socket for the stump, a solid leather strap across his chest and back, and a steel knee-joint that used to give a little click as he swung it forward. It must have been anguish. But we thought it was a wonderful thing and it gave us lots of kudos at school as no-one else's brother provided any such *braggadocio.*

But the thrill of having the hero back began to wear off. Peverley was cross and nervy, frightening the younger children with his gloom and rages. Another sister, Nancy Adrah (or "Ada"), said in 1983: "They went away fighting for king and country and all that. They came back quite disillusioned".

Arthur Edward Albert Hall had sailed from Swansea, Wales, as a land surveyor to work through large tracts of the New South Wales bush late in the nineteenth century, becoming one of the most senior men in the Surveyor-General's Department. Suzy Emma Nancy Foy's father, was a tinker who tethered a cow by the Tank Stream that used to run from the city to Circular Quay. Arthur and Suzy Hall moved from Woollahra to Balmain because they needed a bigger house for their ten children.

The children found Durham House, now the site of Housing Commission flats, an enchanting residence with an elegant staircase leading to the balcony where they slept. An acre of ground with old oak trees and Moreton Bay figs surrounded Durham House, approached by driveways. There was a big stone cellar, a tennis court, and, according to folklore, ghosts. The "silvertails" of Balmain were said to live in Nicholson Street. Barbara Foy wrote:

> Our mother was still a bit of a snob in those days and she had her doubts about Balmain being what she called a lower-class district. She would have liked such a big house in a seemly suburb where we could have met "suitable" friends. Girls, in particular, she felt, shouldn't be mixing with common people, and I seem to have spent my childhood dreaming round the rambling garden, while my lucky brothers were allowed into the hazards and adventures of the working class suburb outside.

The younger Halls were not allowed to go "up Balmain" alone, although some of the boys occasionally crept out at night. Ian Decimus Hall — "Decimus" because he was the tenth child — recalled:

> We were prohibited from going down the bottom of Nicholson Street and playing around there on the wharves and in the water because the old man thought we would be done to death or drowned or carted away on a boat. I remember a Cooper Street gang, a bunch of young kids who never had any money. If they saw a couple of children walking along well-dressed, they'd knock them over because they'd probably have sixpence in a pocket. I lived in fear and trembling of them. Father once stood for the National Party — in a seat almost 100 per cent Labor — and the elder boys went along to meetings to protect him.

Ian Hall remembers crystal sets with "cat's whiskers", a wind-up gramophone, everyone singing round the piano on Friday nights, and the family's old Dodge Tourer, one of the few cars in Balmain at the time: "Father had difficulty with it because, once he'd got it started, he would keep it going regardless of hills, corners or other traffic. My mother sat in the front with trepidation".

Young men and women, mainly from the eastern suburbs, would arrive by ferry on Saturdays to play tennis at Durham House. The young men, mostly law students, wore long cream flannels and white shirts, with well-sleeked hair; sisters and girl friends wore long white skirts with tight, high belts and tucked blouses. Some sons of people whom Mr and Mrs Hall had met at church — and therefore of "good stock" — were also allowed.

Mr Hall was a stern man who loved his children. Like many men of his age, though, he could not show that love. Instead, he encouraged, sometimes drove, them to achieve. All ten won university degrees or diplomas, at a time when few young women sought tertiary education. Ada said: "He was loving and sensitive but he was driven by fear of what would happen to his brood".

Arthur Hall's great spirit, supported by Suzy Em, weakened as the twenties drew to a close. His body was wracked by tuberculosis, a major killer of the day; his mind was troubled as the world slipped into the Great Depression. He would struggle up the Darling Street hill from the ferry to Durham House in the evening when Suzy Em would greet her husband, taking his arm at the front gate. In winter, his pet daughter Barbara would prepare a hot lemon drink and place slippers and clean socks by the fire. She would comfort her father, removing his boots and socks and rubbing his feet,

> . . . so cold, so very white — and then put on the warm socks and slippers. When I think of my father and look back and pity him for the struggle he made out of life, for the love in him that he was afraid to let out, for his serious endeavour to be a "good man" as he knew it, and for the rich brood of children he had that he couldn't enjoy, but only fear for, he seems summed up in those cold, tired, white feet.

Arthur Hall died in 1931, and was buried the day Barbara sat for her final Bachelor of Arts degree examinations of the University of Sydney. A few days later, she found three little children picking snowdrops from the tennis court.

"What do you think you're doing?" demanded Barbara Hall.

"We thought it was empty".

The Halls left soon after. The academic success of the Halls must have been achieved in spite of the school across the street. In the 1930 primary final examination, only five students out of 17 reached 100 marks out of 300. Education Department Archives record that authorities regarded as unsatisfactory the explanation by headmaster George Klein: "The arithmetic paper seemed to awe the children and the majority didn't do it justice".

Klein's successor, Edwin George Christie, complained that a sick teacher had not been replaced: "This school cannot be allowed to suffer even the smallest neglect if its status in the mind of the public is to be rehabilitated and sustained". In the 1931 primary final examinations, only 17 out of 42 passed.

Local residents, however, seemed just as concerned about the game of cricket, which was after all, and has remained, a national pastime. Captain Lancelot E. Lucas had written to the Chief Inspector of Primary Schools at the beginning of 1926 complaining of the "menace" caused by the school's cricket players on their new concrete pitch. The health of the Lucas family was endangered by wildly flying cricket balls, said the captain. Thus began a seven-year battle for the ashes of local schoolboy cricket, perhaps the longest-running issue, apart from that of school funds, to be debated at Nicholson Street.

Headmaster Klein, a cricket fancier, pointed out that cricket balls had occasionally been hit into adjoining properties since the school was opened; that the concrete pitch, laid down by the Parents and Citizens' Association, was less likely to cause trouble than the "bumping pitch" used previously; besides, any boy who hit a six over the fence was out, a sensible provision that had been adopted in crowded suburbs throughout the land.

Netting was installed as a precaution but, in 1927, the Great Cricket Debate had reached the senior levels of the New South Wales Public Service. Mr S.H. Smith, the Under Secretary for Education, ordered that the game be played with a soft ball on weekdays and, if trouble arose from weekend matches, the police should be called.

After more complaints in 1929, acting Under Secretary S. Lasker ordered a full inquiry. Cricket was banned until assurances about safety were given. Headmaster George Klein, questioning the umpire's decision, said the cricket season had ended, another ball would not be bowled for six months and, besides, didn't Mrs Lucas enjoy hosing the boys as they retrieved their balls? Mr Klein, it seems, was also a caring man. He brought the children bags of fruit from his own orchard. Watching the growth of unemployment among youths, he declared they could play cricket in the school grounds outside school hours.

The NSW Education Department's revised decision in 1930 was that cricket could be played only in recesses and with a soft ball and that unemployed youths be banned. Headmaster Christie thought in 1932 that Captain Lucas had a real grievance, having been "exposed to a battery of hoodlums shouting and yelling filth and profanity and trespassing on the premises to play cricket and perpetrate acts of vandalism".

In February 1933, Mr G.R. Thomas, Director of Education, ordered that the pitch be broken up. The end of cricket did not help the academic standards. The results of the 1933 primary final exam showed 15 of the 27 entrants had passed. Christie blamed "previous neglect, faulty teaching and, in some cases, poor mental equipment". Complaints about dangerously flying cricket balls resumed in 1934, even though no formal pitch existed. Trying to ban cricket among young Australians was like trying to ban alcohol among their elders.

Part of the fascination for the game might be explained by the fact Archie Jackson lived in Balmain and his mother was at one time the school's cleaner. The Jacksons came to Balmain from Scotland when Archie was two. By the time the slim, blond boy was 15, he topped the batting averages for Balmain's first grade team; at 17, he played for New South Wales; and at 19 and a year younger than Don Bradman, Jackson played for Australia in 1929. "Boy" Jackson opened with Bill Woodfull against Harold Larwood and Maurice Tate and the Australians were reeling with three wickets lost for 19 before Jackson took charge. He went on to make 164. "Boy" Jackson became known as A.A. Jackson, partly because he adopted his father's name Alexander in pride and partly because it added uniformity to a scorecard where everyone boasted two initials. But he was dead four years later, dismissed by the dreaded TB. In the words of the Bible, he was lovely and pleasant in his life. A.G. "Johnny" Moyes, the critic and broadcaster, wrote: "He flashed across the cricket sky with all the brilliance of a meteor, and before we had fully glimpsed the radiance of his batting he had left us".

The twenties were a stable period in Australian history, offering a breathing space between World War I and the Depression of 1928–1983. Although there were major reforms like the 44-hour week and the introduction of child endowment, the period seems dull in retrospect. Pre-war advances in education had been allowed to stop. There was a swing back to an emphasis on "the three Rs". The *Sydney Morning Herald* editorialised in June 1930:

> Most people are destined to earn their bread in vocations in which no great degree of book-learning is required, and curricula which devote too much attention to purely cultural studies are apt to produce misfits discontented with their lot. In many countries, of late, there has been a reaction against the practice of over-educating the rank and file, that is to say, of equipping them, irrespective of their tendencies and aptitudes, with knowledge which is useless to them in after life and is quickly forgotten.

Dull periods of history often lead people to seek their high moments from such activities as sport. For instance, cultural excitement was virtually non-existent in the 1950s, political thought was barren, Sydney had only a couple of reasonable restaurants and pubs shut at 6 pm for much of the decade. It was in this period that the exploits of a Rugby League team, St George, could stir the blood of Sydneysiders and that the country's athletes, swimmers and tennis players were often featured on newspaper front pages. That is why the death of Jackson came as such a blow to Balmain and Australia in the twenties.

The young, especially the young men, could always expend their energies somehow. Bob Lundie, the son of a Scottish master mariner, was dux of Nicholson Street in 1919. He said in 1983:

> I used to get up at 5 am before school and pull a dinghy around the wharves collecting beer bottles for sale. I'd lead the horse from Murphy's bakery after school or simply pinch coal or wood. I'd clean chimneys or even pump the organ at Saint Mary's before choir practice. Horrie Balkwell and myself even went on strike once because the minister hadn't paid us the 2s 6d owing for a month's pumping and we took off down the aisle with a couple of choristers chasing us.
>
> One teacher told me I was the best Chinaman in the school because I grew the best vegetables — at the bottom of the playground. I had more than one fight stopping kids from pinching my radishes. Nicholson Street was the University of the Painters and Dockers. Mort's Dock employed a thousand of them at one time and many came from the school.

After leaving school, Lundie found his sport in the traditional Balmain way for those days: football in winter, sailing in summer and a fair bit of fighting at any time. After a skirmish in a 1929 yacht race, Lundie's crew actually ambushed Captain Chris Webb's 18-footer *Malvina* as she came round Clarke Island, boarded her and slashed her mainsail to ribbons.

Tony Russell, also from Nicholson Street, was in Lundie's crew that day. On one occassion he was playing League for Balmain against St George in 1928, when a riot broke out after a St George player was flattened. Police had to pull spectators off the playing area. Russell was said by League officials to be "temperamentally unsuited for Rugby League". At Balmain Town Hall a meeting called by team supporters had the decision reversed.

Tony and his brother Mick are said in Balmain to be about the only two men to have scared Les "Leather" Hackett. Hackett was called Leather because he was always throwing this, that is, boxing gloves. He was one of 13 children and it helped to be able to use one's fists in those days. Leather later went on to fight professionally at Leichhardt Stadium. Mick was Australian professional swimming champion and boxed with Les Darcy. All in all, they were a formidable group of young men.

Tony Russell was still in Balmain in 1983, aged 82. He was living in his fifteenth Balmain house. His father was a Spaniard named Rossellio who left home at nine years of age, jumped a sailing ship and ended up in Australia. Later, as Charles Russell, he was caretaker of an old hulk in Mort Bay. Tony's mother, Emily Rosetta Hammond, came from Hobart. The Spaniard and the Tasmanian had eight children. "Things were so bad in one house that my brother Harold woke up to see a rat eating callouses off his feet."

Tony's wife, Henrietta, said: "Everyone was poor but you could leave the front door open. Now you have to lock the toilet".

Tony won a world sailing title in 1945, in *Marjorie II,* a boat he bought for £100. His brother Mick the strong man died soon after, a victim of one of Australia's unhappier claims to distinction. He suffered severe headaches and took up what became a national habit after World War II — headache powders. When he died the doctors said the powders had destroyed his kidneys.

The relative dullness of the twenties did bring the jazz age, the Charleston, and associated attractions. While many Australian clerics were worried about the effect moving pictures might have on their congregations, the good folk of Saint Mary the Virgin's, Balmain, split over the matter of dancing.

Saint Mary's does not have a great record of community involvement. Anglicans among Balmain's leading citizens attended the church in the early days and ministers have always visited homes, hospitals, and schools when it was felt necessary, as well as organising the various, if dwindling, number of clubs that have been part of the church's role in the twentieth century. But the attitude has been more "you're welcome to come to us" than "let us go out to them". One exception came under the auspices of Canon Mervyn Archdall at the turn of the century. Born in Catholic-dominated Eire, he was organising secretary of the London Jews Society, founded Deaconess House in Sydney, ran an alternative high school for some years, fulminated on street corners against "the iniquitous Church of Rome" and against the evils of alcohol. He had some success — the temperance movement persuaded the authorities concerned to introduce 6 pm closing of hotels in 1916.

In 1926, Sydney Willis, a church warden at Saint Mary's, sued Morris Hughes, former secretary of the Sunday school, for the return of certain property, including

Bibles and hymn books. The matter was settled out of court, but deep divisions within the congregation emerged. Dancing was banned in the church hall, locks were changed and there was a struggle between the two sides for the minds of the Sunday school children. Stones and fireworks were thrown at the church during an evening service, the Reverend, F. Kellett was heckled and one hundred people were locked out of the annual parishioners' meeting on the grounds that they had never attended Saint Mary's. According to the minutes of the meeting, ''jazz crazed people rushed the hall doors, almost knocking down the Rector and insulting all who had remained loyal to the Church''. The divisions lingered in 1983.

Durham House, also known as Durham Hall, in Nicholson Street, 1918. Now Housing Commission flats

Arthur Hall and family in his Dodge tourer, about 1928

2nd Class 1921. Valerie Donnelly, who pushed Neville Wran's pram, is the second from the left in the front row

5th Class 1922. The arrow points at Barbara Hall

2nd Class 1922. Eddie Brett is far left second row, Mary West far left third row and Ian Hall is fourth left back row

1st Class 1929

Boxing, swimming, motoring and tennis in the 20s. *(Boxer from the Macleay Museum.) Below* is the staff of Colgate, Tom Hardin is sitting at the rear

2nd Class 1930

Saluting the flag, 1923 at Blackfriars School *(NSW Department of Education)*

Cricket Team, 1930

6th Class 1931

6

"Some people rub you with an indelible mark"

THE DEPRESSION

Edith May Ballerum's husband, Arthur, died during the Depression, aged 47, worrying about the possibility of his engineering business going to the wall and how his family would cope. As a young woman she had made corsets for Madame Paperill in the Strand Arcade but after marriage at 18, she devoted her time to raising five children. With her husband's death, Mrs Ballerum did not know what she would do, until she scraped together enough money to take over a ham and beef shop in East Balmain. Mrs Ballerum said in 1983:

> I'll never forget the Monday morning I opened up for business. Nearly everyone in the East End was crowded around the shop door and out into the street. Nobody had much money but they wanted to help if they could, to give me their support, to buy a small cake or something. It was very moving. They were wonderful people. I decided there and then I would never leave East Balmain.

Mrs Ballerum was 96 in 1983, having lived in Balmain for 91 years.

The years 1928 to 1933 were the worst of a very grim quarter of a century. It wasn't until the late 1930s that real wages returned to the level they had reached before World War I. Then it was time for another war. Unemployment during the twenties was never below seven per cent, a figure surpassed in 1982, when economists were not sure whether Australia was deep in recession or not so deep in depression. They were still not sure in 1983, when the figure reached ten per cent.

There was no doubt about the early thirties — and no doubt that Balmain people were among the hardest hit in the land. In 1933, 27.2 per cent of Balmain breadwinners were unemployed. The figure of the Commonwealth of Australia Census, 1933 for New South Wales was 18.4 per cent.

The *Sydney Morning Herald* said in 1930 that Balmain "feels the pinch acutely, more so perhaps than other suburbs". The newspaper went on that the suburb had ". . . 2,000 children so seriously undernourished as to be in a state of semi-starvation". The *Herald* writer's analysis continued as follows: "Gastro-enteritis carried off babies whom a lack of nourishment deprived of the power of resistance". The paper quoted a few cases:

> There are eight of us and we are living on £1 a week, being the value of rations issued to us. It means that we are each living on 2s 6d a week.

> We have 35s a week coming in. There are 16 of us. The rent is 32s 6d. Nine children are under 14. I cannot get endowment because last year my husband earned £4 over the amount.

> I have a wife and a month old baby. We are left with nothing.

The people of Balmain are traditionally portrayed as having a strong sense of local identity and pride. They are said to be tough, cheerful and self-dependent, and that this might have something to do with peninsularity. There are still some old people who talk of "going to Sydney". That is, they belong to a place, a suburb, rather than a city. Bunky Auland, who went to Nicholson Street School in 1913, likes telling a story about Sir Roderick Miller, the shipper and brewer who lived in Birchgrove, always seen as part of Balmain. Miller would ask himself in convivial company: "What's the centre of the world?"; his shouted reply: "Balmain!" Henry Ballerum, also ex-Nicholson Street and son of Edith May, put it another way: "The greatest religion you could have was to be born in Balmain".

John Kerr, who grew up to become Sir John, Governor-General, and sack Gough Whitlam's elected Labor Government in 1975, was born in Balmain and lived there until 1931. It is doubtful whether he would be welcome there today but he said in 1982: "We always regarded ourselves as being a Balmain family". Kerr's father worked at Mort's Dock with Bill McKell, another Labor man who went on to become Governor-General and kneel before the monarch's sword. Sir William spoke in 1983 about fond memories of battling Balmain. As an apprentice boilermaker young McKell would often have to walk home from Balmain to Redfern at 2 am, after an unpaid overtime shift. McKell and Kerr senior fought for an apprentices' union — and won adult pay. Kerr senior used to fantasise that if he, and not McKell, had put the final case, he might have become a New South Wales Premier and Governor-General.

All these different degrees of affection for, and loyalty to, Balmain were put to a severe test during the Depression. Henry Ballerum recalled:

> I think the Depression killed my father, all that worry about his firm going broke and how his family would survive. He shouldn't have died at 47. We never seemed to have any money, yet I can't remember wanting for anything. Mum started the shop in 1933, opened at 7.30 every morning, stayed open until after the pictures at night and had two hours off every Sunday for church. The unemployed used to gather on the corner of Johnston and Darling Streets, looking out at the Bridge being built and talking. You could see the police coming — a bull-nose Morris chugging up the hill. They just wanted to be sure no one was rioting. But some Balmain families didn't survive. I remember watching the moonlight flits. You'd see a family that couldn't afford the rent any longer pushing a wheelbarrow with their belongings, along Johnston Street, left into Darling Street and away into the night. God knows where they finished up.

Harry Leo did a few moonlight flits. He was one of 11 children born to Michael Patrick and Agnes McGregor Leo. One of the Leo XI, Kathleen, didn't survive the

Depression. A local beauty, she died at 17 of pneumonia and malnutrition. At one stage, because the elder children had married, 18 members of the family were living in the one small terrace. Harry said:

> People slept in the dining room, lounge room and bathroom. We had to boil a copper below ground level and hoist a bucket up the side of the house by rope to the bathroom. I remember my mother making 11 lunches for the family to take to work or to go out and try to get work. She would get up in the morning and make 17 breakfasts. But we ate a lot of porridge, treacle and dumpling stews.
>
> I won the Public Schools Amateur Athletic Association junior sprint when I was about nine and received a pocket. But it wasn't until three years later that we could afford a blazer to put the pocket on. And they couldn't afford running shorts for me. Mum simply sewed a ribbon down the side of my ordinary short trousers.
>
> We didn't even have a radio. Then, in about 1934, my father backed a winner with the SP bookie. He bought a radio — you know, one of those great big ones — and carried it home on his back. He knocked on the front door with his head. We all sat on the floor and listened to the cricket broadcasts. That was terrific fun. We had fun fishing, too, throwing nets in the harbour. There weren't any restrictions those days. We'd share it round the neighbours. You could always get some mussels and put them in a jar. And you could find peaches, pears, locquats, quinces, plums and apricots on trees. Mum would often stew them to make sure they'd last.
>
> I remember rowing out into Mort Bay with Keith McCullough to get a bag of coal from a ship's hold. We needed it to keep warm. Around the end of the Depression I worked for the SP bookie at the back of the Commercial Hotel, running from house to house collecting bets and earning a shilling in the pound commission.

Despite the best endeavours of the children, it was hard to keep a family's heads above water. They would often get behind with the rent. Harry said of the misery of some families:

> We did a midnight flit from Nicholson Street into Johnston Street, just across the road really. I think it was after the worst of the Depression but the houses were wrecks and the owners wouldn't repair anything. We were sitting at dinner one night when plaster from the ceiling hit us all on the head, and fell on to plates. Father had no dinner that night because there was no more food.
>
> Then we did another moonlight flit around the corner to Darling Street. The idea was to arrange it with another family that couldn't keep up with the rent. All you'd have to do was to swap houses. The landlord couldn't do much about it. He knew the departing family couldn't pay any more and he'd hope that the new family would, at least for a few weeks. But I know some families just had to move out of Balmain altogether.
>
> All the Leos would contribute something. I was with the bookie, Jack would

bring home empty beer bottles, Mick was an apprentice electrician screwing in bulbs at Luna Park and would bring home copper wire to sell, Jim worked in a laundry and would bring home unclaimed shirts, the girls worked in the Black and White Milk Bar in Martin Place and used to bring home spare ice cream. It was the only time we'd have ice cream.

Ron Archer, at Nicholson Street during the Depression, said: "One large family used to drain the tea leaves from their pot, put them out in the sun to dry, then use them again for the next pot".

Cicely Curtin, a doctor's wife, said with reference to the poverty experienced by people:

> We had a friend who was a doctor in Balmain at the time. He came to us to say "goodbye". He was going to the country because he couldn't get any money out of the people in his area. All the timber mills down that way closed down. He was only paid six pounds in a whole month!

Dr Hubert "Fuzz" Porter was practising medicine at the time. Born in 1897 and a pupil at the Pigeon Ground School, he became, at 24, the youngest medical superintendent of Sydney Hospital. He said in 1983:

> You could see around 13 patients in a day and not get paid for any of them. The people of Pyrmont and Ultimo were the best payers. The people of Balmain were more likely to pay than those in Drummoyne. I'd operate for nothing at Balmain Hospital. Delivering babies in Balmain during the Depression was pretty crude. People bred a bit faster in those days — I was the eldest of eight. Miscarriages were pretty common, often induced. Women would say that they had fallen down the stairs. Delivering babies at home, it was often hard to find warm water. Baths were used as coal scuttles in a lot of places. The only way I survived as a doctor there was because a tyre manufacturing company took me on a retainer. I knew people who had never missed a day's work in their lives before losing their jobs. They became so discouraged. They would tell you to stuff it.

Colin Hastwell lived next door to the Leos. He said:

> My father used to go out looking for work, come home again and mum would say, "How did you get on today?" He'd say, "Nothing today, but they told me to come back tomorrow". He kept on going back, until he got work. We managed to save our shillings until they became pounds and we bought an old launch and the men used it to earn a living. They went prawning and fishing. I used to go up to Murphy's, the bakers, get the manure and sell it for 3d a bag. And go down to Balmain coal mine and get a railway sleeper for fourpence. We'd get three bags of wood out of them — and sell them for a shilling a bag. People helped one another. The next door neighbour would say, "Everything going all right?" There was no one better than anybody else and that was a good thing.

Alick Braid said:

We used to row across to the wharves where the potato boats came in — spuds and carrots. The police wouldn't get out of their launch if it was raining. We'd split a bag open and everyone in the district would get a share. One day we brought home a bag of sandshoes. The trouble was they were all left feet. Anyhow, we soaked them in water for a while and they were nearly the right shape.

Bob and Irene Snell said the years 1928–33 for them seemed:

An extraordinary time to see the worthiness of mankind in a difficult period. We got together and sang songs and weathered it. There was skulduggery, too. We used to manipulate the gas metre. We used to bypass the register with a rubber hose . . . on weekends when the inspector wasn't around. So mum did all her cooking at weekends and she'd bathe the kids. Steam was coming out everywhere at weekends.

If anyone was going to be evicted, we'd be there. One of our great footballers Chook Fraser (a true Balmain hero who played for Australia) was the personification of compassion and human kindness. He'd shift many an evicted person into another house. One day he'd been invited to watch the visiting English footballers play and he was taking me as a guest. We were hailed by an old man who said, "Mr. Fraser, can you help me? I'm being evicted this afternoon." Chook said, "Well, I'll do my best". So we never got to the football. We shifted the old man's things. Some people just pass you by in life but some, like Chook, rub you with an indelible mark.

We lived on sausages and mince, soup and rabbits at ninepence a pair. Fish augmented the rations. People used to take the lead off the roof and sell it. I lived in one place where they'd taken the lead off. It wasn't so good in the wet.

A team of unemployed young men played in the junior Rugby League competition at Birchgrove in 1933. John Coates, who watched them play, said:

My mother and Frank (her brother) were on the dole and we were in a rented house, 37s 6d a week. The rent was progressively reduced to a pound as things worsened; but we couldn't even meet that. We were threatened with eviction. Frank went to the chamber magistrate and put his case. The magistrate said, "Make an offer". So Frank offered a shilling — one shilling a week! The owner was ordered to accept and we stayed. This way we were not refusing to pay. The old landlord came for the back rent every Saturday morning until about 1940 and he was finally squared up.

We young 'uns of that era left much of the militancy to the older men, I'm afraid. We didn't have the New Guard in Balmain much. We were more worried about the likes of Sir Otto Niemeyer, the emissary from the Bank of England who cracked the whip in Canberra. The only one to effectively oppose him was Jack Lang.

Balmain also has a reputation for being of a fairly radical bent. Yet the radicalism tends to stay below the surface. Up until recently Balmain representatives on Leichhardt Council were usually the most conservative Labor type. Even in the Depression, radicalism rarely looked like turning into rebellion.

Discontent did, however, surface in the classroom. It is recorded in NSW Education Department Archives that Mrs R. Crow complained in 1931 Miss Goulding had flogged Leslie, her boy of five years "so unmercifully as to bring out great bruises and marks". Mrs Crow said her husband was unemployed and "this crime merits summons for assault". Headmaster Christie said the boy threw a slate at Miss Goulding, hitting her in the face, causing her mouth to bleed and her glasses to break: "The boy's father made it very plain to me that he regarded it as his duty to teach his son to defend himself against authority as constituted by a corrupt and capitalistic society". Miss Goulding said she had simply slapped the child.

Christie wrote to Inspector George Back: "No one knows better than yourself the inscrutable nature of child psychology and the danger of positive opinions on child behaviour . . . His father is a militant communist seized with the fanaticism of teaching his boy the only true religion". Miss Goulding was exonerated and Empire Day celebrations followed soon after, with much saluting of the flag and a program interspersed with song and poetry. Sweets were handed out to infants.

In the 1931 federal elections, Labor candidates were opposed by Lang Labor men, supporters of New South Wales Premier Jack Lang, who led opposition to the English bankers and the national policy decided at the pre-election Premiers' Conference. In Dalley, the seat which included Balmain, Ted Theodore, Treasurer in the Scullin Government, was beaten by Rosevear, a Lang supporter. Theodore's defeat might have had something to do with the fact that, asked the reason he did not live in his electorate, he answered: "A man may work in the abattoirs, but that is no reason why he should live in the abattoirs". There was also a strong positive vote for Lang.

The Balmain Unemployed Workers' Movement, led by Jack Sylvester, held meetings from 1930. Sylvester's group broke from the Communist Party in 1933, when a new communist unemployed group was founded in Balmain by Stan Moran, the Domain orator who later bestowed on Prime Minister Robert Menzies the name "Pig Iron Bob". Few people in 1983 remembered the UWM, but they represented an attempt by the unemployed to control their own lives.

Nick Origlass, the old hand of Balmain politics, said in 1983: "They were attacking Jack Lang. While he had massive support, they were biting at his heels". Stan Moran was still living at Rozelle in 1983 and singing a Depression song to his grandchildren:

I was born long ago in 1894, I've seen many a crisis I will own,
I've been hungry, I've been cold, and now I'm growing old,
But the worst I've seen is 1934.
Oh, those beans, bacon and gravy, they nearly drive me crazy,
I eat them till I see them in my dreams, in my dreams,
But I wake up in the morning, another day is dawning,
And I know I'll have another plate of beans!

There were fights, but violence never lasted. The Right-wing New Guard, which had been moving into various suburbs, were driven out by flailing fists when they tried to break up a meeting at Rozelle. And Constable Elton S. Lewis, a church warden at Saint Mary's, had to draw his pistol to help stop disturbances among 5000 unemployed at The Domain in 1930.

The building of the Bridge provided the gold among these black days. The children of Nicholson Street had a grandstand view, watching the arches come together day by day. Headmaster Klein would march the children out into the playground every now and then to point out the latest advance, just in case they had missed it. Billo Robinson ferried construction materials to the bridge site; John McKee, still living in Balmain, worked as a rigger on it, along with dozens of other Balmain men; and all the children marched over the Bridge the day it opened.

Some of the marchers claim it was on this day that Nicholson Street became known as ''Nicholly High'' — because the children marched behind the students of Fort Street and wanted themselves on a more equal footing with that illustrious school. But the ''Nicholly High'' tag goes back at least to the first decade of the twentieth century. It might have had something to do with the fact that the school is perched high on the Balmain ridge; or that children from Nicholson Street often completed their schooling there, whereas other students finished their formal education at a high school; or it might have been the brainwave of a long forgotten girl or boy with a sardonic taste in humour.

Colin Hastwell fell out of a tree the day the Bridge opened, suffering concussion. And the next day Eunice Weldon, now Mrs Hemsley, thought she would go one better than her young friends who had walked across. Eunice and her brother, Ray, climbed right over the main arch. ''They stopped people doing it after that. They thought it was too dangerous''.

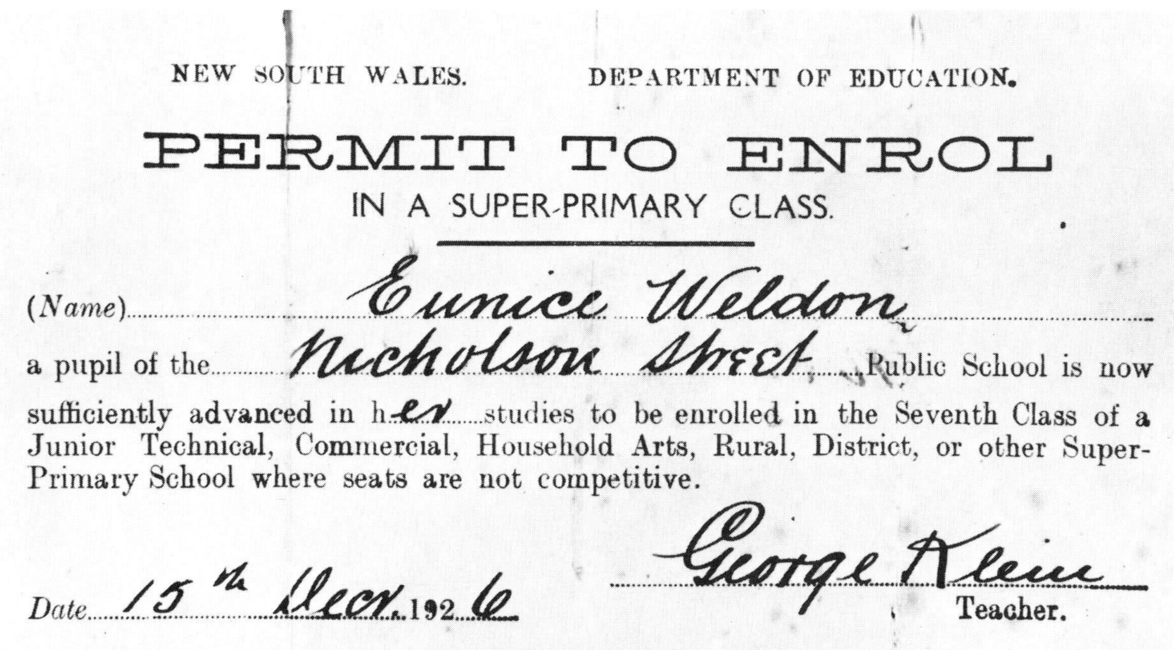
NEW SOUTH WALES. DEPARTMENT OF EDUCATION.

PERMIT TO ENROL

IN A SUPER-PRIMARY CLASS.

(*Name*) Eunice Weldon

a pupil of the Nicholson Street Public School is now sufficiently advanced in her studies to be enrolled in the Seventh Class of a Junior Technical, Commercial, Household Arts, Rural, District, or other Super-Primary School where seats are not competitive.

George Klein
Teacher.

Date 15th Decr. 1926

Agnes McGregor Leo, matriarch of the Balmain Leos

Balmain unemployed workers march in the Depression

Late 1920s funeral procession in Darling Street *(Macleay Museum)*

Classic Harold Cazneaux photo of the joining of the Harbour Bridge arch

7

"Balmain boys don't cry"

THE WRANS

Neville Wran is the best-known former student of Nicholson Street School. He has also been one of Australia's most successful post-war politicians. He led the New South Wales Labor Party to Government in May 1976, only six months after Sir John Kerr, also born in Balmain, had traumatised Labor supporters by sacking Gough Whitlam's Federal Labor Government.

In May 1976 the swing to Wran was such that a new word was added to the political lexicon — "Wranslide". Wran was the man to lead the people of New South Wales, said the slogans. Wran's the Man.

His critics say he is short on political philosophy, other than having a perfect grasp of the fact that politics is all about having power, he doesn't always think through what can or should be done with that power and that, when he does use it, it is as likely to be in the interests of forces opposed to good old traditional Labor ideals. However, he has an acute sense of what the public wants, how far he can go, how much change they will tolerate. Opinion in May, 1978, once put his acceptance by the public at an extraordinary 80 per cent. It had slipped by 1983 but, despite the Street Royal Commission of that year, Wran still led the Opposition's Nick Greiner in an opinion poll published in the *Bulletin* in July. The Labor Party still looked like the established governing party in New South Wales.

The Royal Commission was set up to inquire into allegations that Murray Farquhar, a former Chief Stipendiary Magistrate, had sought to influence the course of justice in a case involving Rugby League chief Kevin Humphreys, another Balmain boy. NSW Chief Justice Sir Laurence Street was asked to decide whether Wran had brought pressure on Farquhar.

It was a trying time for Neville Wran, the first time a Premier had been placed in such a position. He stepped aside from his post for the duration of the commission. He told the Labor Party's conference that some of the mud thrown at him would stick but "Balmain boys don't cry. We're too vulgar and too common for that and probably vote Labor anyway". He added, paraphrasing Shakespeare's *The Merchant of Venice:* "But if you prick us with a pin we bleed like anyone else and I can assure you that the stress, anguish and indignity of the past two weeks have been extraordinary, and a unique experience for me".

Asked in the commission by Maurice Neil, counsel for Farquhar, what he understood by the phrase "old Balmain boy", Wran replied: "Balmain used to have a quiet, village atmosphere, a good community atmosphere''. He said ''old Balmain boy'' was an honourable folklore phrase. Street exonerated Wran, while judging that Farquhar had influenced the Humphreys case.

Wran sometimes returns to Balmain, mainly to eat some fish and drink some beer with his brother Joe. He loves talking about the place. The contrast between Wran the polished political performer on television and Wran the raconteur of Balmain tales is fascinating. There's a touch of the larrikin to the latter. It sometimes spills over in Parliament.

He thinks he owes his background a good deal. He also takes pride in the fact that its harshness was never allowed to grind his family down, like it did other families. Most of his old schoolmates remember him fondly and with admiration, although some thought of him as ''an egghead'' and others laughed because he was ''a hopeless football player''.

Neville Wran's mother, Lillian Langley Wran, came from a working-class family in Waverley but there were Wrans in Balmain well back into the nineteenth century. His great grandfather was a stonemason-sculptor, believed to have worked on some of the GPO and Lands Department carving. Joe Wran said that his great grandparents settled on some land, known as Wran's Paddock before becoming Pilcher's Paddock, now the site of the White Bay container terminal. Joe and Neville's grandfather was also a stonemason. Joe said he was a ''great tippler'' who had fallen from a horse-drawn cab and lost a leg. Neville said: ''Regrettably he got drunk and fell under a carriage and lost his legs — which made it a bit awkward to go up a ladder''. The Premier, however, conceded that his elder brother had a more precise grasp of family history.

The Premier also recalled an uncle recognised as something of a character around Balmain:

> My uncle was incarcerated on the *Sobraon.* He dived overboard and escaped and was secreted by his brothers and taken to a farm on the heights of Pymble, quite an epic journey apparently. Uncle George — great old fellow — was naturally wrongly convicted of stealing a whip from a carriage. He was a larrikin; he went through a lot of women, always had a new wife. I used to be told as a kid, ''This is Uncle George's a new wife''. Dreadful old womaniser.

The first house he remembers is 117 Darling Street, a little terrace just around the corner from The Avenue. Architect James McDonald designed the house, which was begun in 1891. A sign of the times was that, by a separation of the stairs into two steep wings, the architect was able to isolate the servant's quarters from the family bedrooms. Lillian and Joseph Wran had eight children including Neville, the youngest — there was no room for servants. The Wrans later rented a house from Harry West, the sailmaker, at 11 Nicholson Street.

Joe Wran, 75 in 1983 and about 18 years older than his brother, was the only member of the family still living in Balmain — in the same Campbell Street house he had occupied since his marriage in 1929. Joe was ''sick of being learned'' by the time he was 11. He thought he was better off learning to work. So he helped on a fruit cart until, at the age of 16, he bought a horse for £5, hired a harness and cart for 4s a day and drove off to start his own business. He built up a round in Balmain and Rozelle but the Depression values were taking hold. He extended his round to take in Double Bay on two days of the week. The secret, he said, was in the buying. "If you buy good potatoes and beans, you're half-way there". Hundreds tried their hand at the job during the Depression, but most went broke. There were four fruit-and-vegetable carters in Balmain at one stage. Once, for some light relief, the four salesmen held a race from the Commercial Hotel in the East End, up Darling Street, around the war monument in Loyalty Square and back.

Joe Wran thought Drummoyne, though superficially quite prosperous, was poorer than Balmain in the Depression, a theory supported by Dr Porter. Young married couples had gone to the fashionable new brick cottages in Drummoyne only to find they couldn't afford the 37s a week rents. They would eat bread and treacle between pay days, all behind a veneer of middle-class upward mobility. "Never been a good shop in Drummoyne," said Joe. "Never could support a good shop". Balmain was different; the poverty more visible and the social networks more supportive. People helped one another when in trouble — and there were lots of people in trouble.

The Landlord and Tenant Act kept rents down. But Joe, who paid 15s a week to his land lady, was the only tenant still paying the rent to her. She came round to check that he could afford it. "No one else can," she said. He bought the house after World War II. He also bought a 1932 Chevrolet truck for £37 10s and carried on the fruit and vegetable business until the 1960s, by which time his younger brother had established a reputation as a formidable lawyer, especially in the industrial relations area. "A real afterthought," Joe said of Neville. "But a smart one. I wouldn't want his job for quids but, then, he always liked things difficult . . . got bored if things were easy when we were being reared".

Joe and Neville Wran's father had several different jobs during his lifetime, including that of a coal lumper on the 60 milers, the ships that travelled mainly between Sydney, Newcastle and Port Kembla. He was shipwrecked once off Fort Denison when his ship was hit by a bigger vessel and one man drowned.

> A Manly ferry picked them up and, instead of taking them back to Balmain, the bloody Manly ferry took them to Manly. It was cold and, of course, they got down in the stoke hold to get warm. And by the time they got to Manly, making out in the pub as heroes, the inevitable happened. They all got drunk. They eventually got home about 9 o'clock next morning and told the story to my mother who just wouldn't have a bar of it.
>
> He was a seaman but, in the Depression he did what he could, mainly getting jobs at Chapman's Engineering and Mort's Dock. Then he got a job as a cleaner at the old Theatre Royal; then as supervisor of Her Majesty's building, which was a big break for me because it meant we got free tickets to all the shows.

Later, while studying law, Wran was a member of the Sydney University Dramatic Society. He said: "Acting puts you beyond embarrassment. It teaches you how to use the furniture of a courtroom or a parlour — what you've got''. But he is glad he chose the law rather than the stage. ''I would have been a second-rate actor'' he was reported as saying in the *Sydney Morning Herald,* on 16 October 1982.

Before the stage, the youngest Wran had tried the boxing ring at a boys' club. ''Someone got me into a boxing ring and punched me in the nose. I decided then and there that it wasn't for me. I changed from boxing to basketball that afternoon. Upheaval is not my style at all — that's a reflection on the punch in the nose I got''.

A favourite schoolboy pastime was raiding fruit trees. ''There was this dreadful woman in Nicholson Street who made it a greater challenge. She had quite a big property and if she caught you she took your pants off and kept your pants, so you had to go home without them which was, in those days of higher levels of morality, the ultimate disgrace''.

Did he ever get caught? ''No, I never did, but a lot of my friends did. They don't call me Nifty for nothing''.

Charley Middleston did get caught. Charley began at Nicholson Street in 1926 and admitted in 1983 that he'd had some problems with discipline.

> The teacher would say, ''Three cuts on the left hand and three on the right, or do you want them all on the one hand?'' We did some terrible things, like blowing up letter boxes. The girls would join up with the boys around cracker night. Blowing up letter boxes was a special and in those days they had really snazzy crackers. A basket bomb would blow half the bloody house out.
>
> Anyhow, I remember David McFarlane saying to me, ''Those pears are ripe at old Ma Webb's. So after school we got up the tree. Lo and behold! Who do you think comes round the corner but old Ma Webb and her two cattle dogs. ''I got you pair of buggers and I know you young Middleton. You'll have to take your pants off and throw them down here because you are not going home without I get your pants''. So we had to take our pants off, climb down and run home naked. Mrs. Webb told the story in the butcher's shop. Well, the whole bloody mob roared their heads off. So she said to mum, ''You send him up and I'll give them to him''.

The children of Balmain at this time played hockey on roller skates in the street and cricket with banana boxes as the wicket. Boys and some girls swam in the harbour off Darling Street wharf. The more daring would climb on to a ferry and jump off into the wash as it pulled out for the Erskine Street wharf. They would ''shoot the breeze'' (chat in the fresh air) down near the wharf and make fish traps. Wran recalled rowing a dinghy with Ron Robinson to White Bay,

> fishing and messing around, untieing a few people's moorings and letting their boats go, just to be jolly good citizens.
>
> We could always catch crabs down at the bottom of The Avenue, blue swimmers. Sometimes my dad would say, ''Why don't you go and get us a bag of mussels?'' You'd go and get a sugar bag full of mussels. I thought they were superb times. We used to grease sheets of galvanised tin and slide down the

gutters of The Avenue, down to the Adelaide Steamship Company.

But I do remember some bad times. To this day I can remember seeing one mother pour hot water on her kid's crispies. That was his breakfast — crispies and hot water — that soggy bloody mess. I was probably the only kid in the school who had a pair of shoes. Not probably, I was. A brother who is dead would go out and catch 24 tailer — sometimes he would catch none — but when he caught them my mum would take enough for us and distribute them to all the people around, so everbody got a feed. Lots of people did that. Now nobody cares whether you have a feed or not. I remember going on Joe's horse and cart down to the market. Great fun. The first time I ate a salami roll. A delicacy. You could get threepence worth of ham or beef at Ballerum's shop — not cut thick.

Mrs Ballerum remembered the young Wran buying a penny lolly, too: "He was a dear child, so soft in his way. He was the boy who took my eye".

Wran said:

It was pretty hard to get a job. That is why I'm a bit worried about the people now. I think there is going to be a lot of unemployment here, and I don't think we are geared psychologically to take it. We've all taken everything for granted for so long. I don't know how we'll go when the bloody belt comes in.

We used to do lots of things to get money. I used to run a sweep on the 18-footers. Get on the ferry, make a few bob. An alderman used to give us threepence to deliver his dodgers (pamphlets). We'd deliver them to one street and use the rest for toilet paper. The old man used to walk from Balmain to Circular Quay because a bloke there would give better weight for the meat. Imagine walking, but we had nothing to do, see.

Mobile vendors were popular in the thirties, even a man who carved meat from a side of beef at the front gate. The rabbitoh used to come round. Your mum would pick which pair of rabbits she'd have — she'd go through a dozen of them — and the guy would behead and skin them and gut them in five minutes. You wouldn't buy them unless that ritual was gone through. People would come round selling clothes props. There were the usual poor sods who couldn't get a job and who'd have a handful of neckties or pots and pans.

Then there was Arty Beaumont. He smoked fish. He only smoked enough to get a drink. That's all he was interested in and, if you didn't get Arty before he sold the first basket, you didn't get any fish that weekend. He would get into that little pub and that would be the end of Arty. But nobody smoked fish like Arty before or since . . . beautiful.

There was a milk and egg man, too, who had the hide to run over my Pomeranian dog. To punish him we let his tyres down every time he came into the street after that, which rather incommoded him.

He doesn't remember having gone hungry:

Not ever. No. We were too good for that, because we could fish and were never short of coal. There were plenty of coal stacks around Mort's Dock. Plenty of wood. Joe sold fruit and vegetables three days a week through the Depression; the other days he'd sell fish. We had plenty of both. I can remember this big copper in — it wasn't called the laundry — the washhouse, with 10 or 12 lobsters crawling around. He'd keep them lined up until he was ready to pop them in the copper and sell them.

We loved bread and dripping. Fried bread. We put the dripping on top after that. Yet I remember being in demand at play time because some children would vie to have my apple core. You'd grown spinach and lettuce and things like that in the backyard.

But some of the kids were very badly kept. I can remember kids with fungus in their ears — wax when it goes green, and kids with green on their feet. Their parents were very neglectful.

Wran remembered Gertrude Goulding, the schoolteacher who maintained discipline at Nicholson Street during the Depression:

I thought she was tough. She would terrorise you and then you had to stand there singing "I'm H-a-p-p-y". You'd feel you were from Belsen or Dachau or somewhere, and you'd have to sing "I'm h-a-p-p-y, I know I am I'm sure I am . . ." My great contribution in the school play was as a chook. Mum made me a black crepe paper costume. I went as a black orpington and a girl I know went as a white leghorn.

It was a very physical environment in those days. I could never fight but I had to fight a couple of blokes just to show that I was all right — I hated it. There was a fight every afternoon, out the back by the side of the school. You had to take your turn to have one. It was bloody awful. Sometimes you'd get a hiding.

Wran's schoolmates remember that he was less inclined to sport than most young men, more intellectual. Harry Leo said:

I told him I would teach him to play football if he would teach me to be a scholar. I used to kick a ball to him and we sat down and he tried to show me where I was going wrong. He couldn't play football, but I think he had the hardest job of the two of us. We used to race marbles down the gutter in Paul Street — a halfpenny in, the winner take all — but Neville wouldn't be in that sort of thing.

Ron Isberg, whose father died from the effects of mustard gas poisoning and who was in Wran's class, said: "He was too good for us at bloody school. Nicholly High produced hundreds of painters and dockers and hundreds of shipwrights, but only one lawyer that I know of".

Colin Hastwell: "I remember this chap who always had his hand up first with the answer. We'd be outside playing cricket and this boy, perhaps one or two others, would still be working away inside".

Other Wrans were more proficient with their fists. Doug, an elder brother now dead, fought what Neville called,

> the best fist fight that was ever fought in Balmain. He fought a bloke called Cornie, one of the local bullies. The fight started at the top of Duke Street (up on the Balmain ridge) and they belted hell out of one another right down to Mort Bay. My brother knocked him half unconscious and then stood on him in the water. They got my brother off him. Cornie regrettably lived.
>
> My father also fought a great fist fight in Pilcher's Paddock, where the container terminal now is. My mother could see from the verandah in Darling Street — the crowd and these two figures hammering away. It was my dad, having a joust with Limerick O'Connor, an amateur champion of Australia. My dad beat him, too. They were a bit angry with each other at the time but they all went out and got drunk the next day and made up. There was a good deal of fighting. I think it was because people had to get it out of their systems somehow. A lot of it was because people didn't have much to do.
>
> Kids generally were much more disciplined by their parents. I wouldn't dare speak disrespectfully to my mother. She was quite the matriarch, the old girl. Very intelligent, tough old bird. She had eight kids and looked after them all well. But my sisters, for instance, dare not come home late. If they were told to be in by 10 o'clock, they were in by bloody 10 o'clock. If they weren't, my mother was waiting half-way up the street. She would come for the bloke as well as the sister! They had this lack of inhibition about their brood. They didn't mind a bit of public display, which would embarrass us today.
>
> There were totally different standards of behaviour in those days. I don't think women's freedom has made men more respectful of them. You couldn't swear in front of a woman. My dad? No way.

Alick Braid remembered one of the Wran women, Dorothy, one of Neville's sisters, more than the rest of the class: "She was called 'Dossie' and we thought she was an angel. She was a picture".

It was because of Dorothy Wran that Valerie Donnelly met the boy who would be Premier. Valerie's great-great grandparents were Prussians who were among the first settlers in the Barossa Valley and whose blood was mixed with some wild Irish. She started making her own clothes in the Depression. In 1983 she was still making dresses — rather more expensive lines — for a boutique she ran in Sydney's Wentworth Hotel. But, before then, Valerie Donnelly used to visit Dossie Wran and push the boy in his pram. "Yes, he was a nice boy," she said. "John Kerr was a handsome young fellow, too".

Another Wran girl, Lillian, thought all Wran children owed a lot to their "wonderful parents", who gave their brood love and firmness. Lillian, who became Mrs Robyns, recalled Neville's first day at school: "He came home and said he didn't think he liked it much. Mother said, 'Yes you will, my boy'". The mother had aspirations for her children which were probably beyond those of most Balmain parents of the time. They were reflected in many ways, some of which can seem quaint today. The girls, for instance, wore gloves and hats when they went out. Lillian attended the Pigeon Ground school and was once called out at assembly as an example of how girls should dress. "I still wear gloves when I go out," said Lillian Robyns, "and I carry them in summer".

In 1983 the Premier of New South Wales joked about not being able to afford to buy Onkaparinga, a Balmain home restored to its two-storey, sandstone magnificence after having been divided into flats and called "Cockroach Castle". It was bought in 1982 by Malcolm Young, of the pop music group AC/DC, for about $900 000. That's not working class money. "I reject the term 'working class'," said Wran in a report published by the *Sydney Morning Herald,* 19 June 1982.

> I'm more working class now than ever I was. Just because I don't drop my "aitches" all the time and spit on the floor while eating my lunch doesn't mean I'm not working class. Everyone aspires to do a little better. That's what being in the working class is all about — how to get out of it.

Neville Wran's father, Joseph. Member of the Royal Naval Reserve and coal lumper

Joe Wran

Sold . . . the Wran house, 117 Darling Street, 1982

Neville Wran, about four and *right* Neville Wran, about nine. With niece Yvonne

Neville Wran, Sydney University Dramatic Society days and *right* Neville Wran, budding lawyer. With sister Lillian

1st Class 1931. Neville Wran is in front of the drainpipe

Classes of 1933. Neville Wran second right in back row, with Harry Leo to his right and Ron Robinson to his left

Premier Wran in 1982 with another Balmain identity, former NSW Premier and Governor-General Sir William McKell *(John Fairfax and Sons)*

Three famous former Nicholson Street pupils; Neville Wran, Wee Georgie Robinson and Wayne Pearce

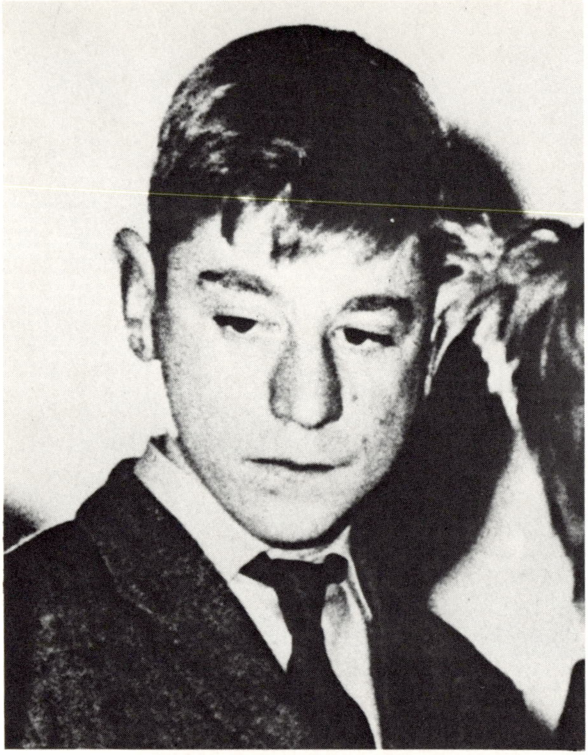

Unknown boy who was taken in by a Balmain family, then went to World War II to be killed in action

Balmain League team that toured Queensland by rail

8

"War does funny things to people"

WORLD WAR II

Children of New South Wales schools who attended the sesquicentenary celebrations of the landing of Captain Arthur Phillip in Sydney at the Sydney Showground in 1938 might have wondered about the accuracy of the history they were being taught. Just emerging from the Depression, they sang of prosperity. With the black clouds of war looming again over Europe, they sang of peace. What's more, the children of Nicholson Street School were dressed as Aboriginals, a group of people who had seen little peace or prosperity since the white man arrived to make a colony 150 years previously. The sentiments of their song were based more on hope than on fact:

One hundred years have passed away,
and then some fifty more,
Since Phillip on that fateful day,
first landed on our shore.
He landed in Port Jackson,
unfurled the flag we love;
Then found an earthly paradise,
and called it Sydney Cove.
City of golden sunlight,
Sydney by the sea;
Open all your portals wide,
to peace — prosperity.
Regal in all your splendour,
gem of the Empire's crown;
Queen city of our nation,
Sydney town!

The words of the song show that the old blend of empire loyalty and bourgeois virtues was still a dominant force in the education system. One lesson of that day was that the song should be allowed to die a quick death. It sunk without trace.

Two young boys gained another advantage from the celebrations. They were Ron Archer, who had shared a classroom with Neville Wran, and Joe Leo, one of the ubiquitous Leos. (By 1983, nearly 270 descendants had sprung from the union in 1910 of Michael and Agnes Leo and, according to son Harry, they were all still talking to one another.) Ron Archer and Joe Leo wore their imitation Aboriginal costumes from the sesquicentenary celebrations when they sang carols outside Balmain pubs during the Christmas of 1938. There had been 33 pubs in Balmain in 1931 and most survived to 1938. Archer and Leo made a "small fortune" with their carols. By the next Christmas, Australia was at war again.

Fewer Balmain men enlisted this time. Many were in protected jobs, manning the wheels of industry which were turned towards the war effort. Once again the women bore the brunt of keeping the families on the rails. Girls left school early to help. The thinking of the time is reflected by the extraordinary words of a poem entered in a sesquicentenary competition:

Ye girls of British race,
Famous for your beauty;
Breed fast in all your grace,
For this is your duty.
As Anzac gave in war,
So daughters at your call,
Will quick respond the more
To replace those that fall.

Ron Archer's brother, Noel, also went to Nicholson Street. The two trace their ancestors back to a Portuguese boy called Freuger, who, according to the family story, was picked up by the missionary ship *John Williams* in the nineteenth century, when he was about to be eaten by Pacific Island cannibals. He was brought to Australia, where he assumed the name Fragar. A granddaughter, Emma Matilda Fragar, married Jack Hand, an engine driver from England and the couple moved to Balmain, opening a paper shop. Emma's daughter, Alma, married Jesse Archer, a master mariner from England who survived the sinking of his merchant ship in World War I to settle in Australia.

Alma's son Ron went to Fort Street Boys' High School about the same time as Wran but left to go to sea when he was 14. Arriving home from New Guinea on leave, at the Darling Street wharf he saw trenches dug in the adjoining Thornton Park. Walking up Clifton Street to his home, he noticed air raid shelters in the school playground. The big house on three-quarters of an acre (0.3 ha) of land was boarded up. "Your parents have moved to Hurlstone Park," a neighbour told him. "They thought it was safer". They had sold up for £1140 after the Japanese submarines had slipped into Sydney Harbour. The youth accepted if philosophically. "After all, I was eating better at sea than I had as a kid. I remembered my mother buying a 2s 6d pullover from Coles at Rozelle, with cotton sleeves and collar sewn on to make it look like a shirt. I'd never used toilet paper until I went to sea — it was usually the telephone directory". And he remembered the days when children would take the school inkwells and throw them at the rent collector. Ron Archer became Australia's youngest master mariner at 23, sailing Rod Miller's ships. In 1983 he was sailing Sydney ferries.

Noel Arena's war experience was just as enlightening for a young man. His father Domenico and mother Josephine had come from Italy and helped put Sydney's fishing industry on a commercial footing. They settled in the house near the school once occupied by Captain Banks. The 50 ft (15 m) ballroom was used to repair fishing nets. The Arenas caught squid, bream, whiting and flathead from the harbour wall and more fish from their boats, selling most, giving some away to the needy. But he was called a ''dago'' at school. He said:

> I felt it. I went out of my way to develop an Australian accent. I avoided speaking Italian. Then, when I joined the AIF, it was completely different. I was accepted. I bear no grudges. My kids were accepted. In the end the locals were attending dances in our ballroom. And mum was making lamingtons for the dancers.

Balmain was like any other suburb at the time — racism hung in the streets. The windows of shops run by Continentals were stoned. Greeks, also called ''dagos'', placed signs in their windows pointing out they were not Italians. Most of the older families appear to have defended the migrants who were bringing a rich new texture to the social fabric, but those old British Empire ideals taught in the schools hadn't catered for the newcomers.

Gaetano Messina had come in 1906 from the islands south of Italy to start a new life in Australia. He was interested in amateur theatricals and he had a brother who was a cellist. The brother chose the United States of America. Gaetano and his wife settled into a mixed business in Balmain, he became known as Tom, they had children and worked hard. Older people remember Mrs Messina feeding soup to the unemployed during the Depression. Those not so old remember her son Jack, a machinist at Goat Island, playing Father Christmas there. Jack joined up during the war — and his father was interned, one of the cruellest ironies to befall any family. Frank ''Rigger'' Martin, whose father, ''Oysters'' Martin, was gassed in World War I, and who has lived in Balmain for all of his 55 years, said:

> The Messinas were a nice family and Pop was a real old gentleman. He used to talk a bit about how Mussolini had cleaned the beggars off the streets and cut down on prostitution — you know the sort of thing, like getting the trains to run on time. A lot of people said similar things about Mussolini. Jack had been born in Australia and it was natural enough for him to enlist. The Messinas had been in Balmain longer than many families. How they could lock up the old man was hard to understand.

Santa Messina, a daughter still living in Balmain in 1983, didn't like to talk about it, apart from saying that many old Balmain people had made wonderful stands on their behalf. ''War does funny things to people,'' she said. ''Politics makes enemies of people. It's not the people themselves''.

George Mimis owned a grocer shop on the corner of Darling and Johnston Streets and several homes in the area. He was Armenian, but known by some locals as ''The Turk''. The rationing of food and other goods began from 1942. This was because war had restricted imports along the normal shipping lanes and the Japanese capture of

Java had cut the supply of tea. On top of this, drought showed that it could wreak its havoc at any time, war or peace. Tea was supposed to be rationed to half a pound (227g) per person every five weeks. This worked out at about two cups a day. People started drinking tea that was very weak. Tea rationing was tightened even further towards the end of the war, by which time butter, sugar, meat and clothing were also rationed.

The introduction of such restrictions inevitably brings a counter-attack. The people who are restricted seek ways of breaking the regulations. Such is human nature. There were ways around prohibition in the United States in the 1920s and there were ways around paying tax in Australia early in the 1980s. During the war, Australians found ways around the rationing system — either because they were needy or because they were greedy. The "black market" system quickly evolved and became an open secret. Frank "Rigger" Martin said:

> In the Depression we used to row over to the wharves and get anything that was going — a bag of potatoes, anything. The police would turn a blind eye to it, within reason. We once swam a pig across Johnston's Bay — just pulled him behind our boat. In the war many families found it hard to exist on their ration books. If they had the money they could pick up extra food from various black markets. You could get black market butter from George Mimis. It all sounded reasonable enough. He wore a big white apron and you'd stand and watch him slice the butter up from a big slab, or cut the bacon off the bone.

George Mimis is also remembered for an act of strength. The tram used to run down the steep Darling Street hill to the wharf by means of a counterweight system, which prevented tram and passengers from being flung into Darling Harbour. The tram would link up at the top of the hill with a four-wheel truck known as the dummy, which was connected to a heavier counterweight under the tracks. When the counterweight went uphill, the tram and dummy were eased down; when the tram went back up, it was pulled by the counterweight coming down. Boys and girls from Nicholson Street delighted in jumping on and off the dummy, at considerable risk to their necks. One day a boy fell under the dummy, trapping a leg. Mimis lifted the dummy, allowing the boy to be dragged free, albeit with a crippled leg.

War also brought differences among local workers. Nick Origlass, an ironworker at Mort's Dock, remembers tradesmen, wearing hats, walking up one side of the street from work while other ranks of the workforce, hatless, took the other side of the street. Origlass, who was to be expelled from the Labor Party 30 years later for his opposition to the party's decision to approve the building of a chemical farm in the area, had been an active communist during the war. When Stalin took the side of those opposing Hilter and Mussolini, the Communist Party enthusiastically endorsed the war effort. Origlass, expelled from the Communist Party, joined the Communist League, which "horrified soldiers in the Domain with banners proclaiming 'Down with Imperialist War'". The battle between the two communist groups reached dramatic heights at Mort's Dock with a six-week strike over which group controlled the union delegates. Origlass said the waterfront strike was "unprecedented as a strike against officials — not the boss". The strike also led to fist fights between the communists and other workers.

War took its toll on the schools. Signs of a revival in the education system were delayed for a decade while the matters that appeared of more immediate urgency were being decided. The schools threw themselves behind the war effort.

More than 1500 teachers and departmental officials enlisted and extra women teachers were appointed. More than £1 300 000 was raised by the schools in the state of New South Wales. Girls and boys knitted more than 61 000 pairs of socks and 29 000 mufflers, made 30 000 camouflage nets, and collected 225 tons of aluminium and other metals, 1 450 tons of rubber, and half a million books and magazines.

John McKee, had come from Glasgow in 1926, helped build the Sydney Harbour Bridge, walked the Hungry Mile looking for a wharf labourer's job during the Depression, and worked on the electrification of the railway line from Redfern to Strathfield. He recalled:

> I remember the air raid trenches dug at the bottom of Darling Street. When the Japanese subs were found in the harbour there were searchlights everywhere that night. We put the two kids under the dining room table and went out to have a look. There were people, kids, everywhere in the street and down by the water.

The Parents' and Citizens' Association at Nicholson Street, which had caused the electric light to be disconnected in 1937 by its "dilatoriness in not affecting the necessary adjustments to the installation", picked up its game in 1939 and introduced a "social and dance" every fortnight.

Some dangers were more of a local nature. Allan Buckley, P and C Association secretary, wrote in 1941 to Clive Evatt, Minister for Education, expressing a "desperately urgent" need for the school to have breathing space. Buckley asked for more land and for a shark-proof swimming pool at Simmons Point. "Children are at present only allowed into shark infested waters," he warned. Baker added: "We believe we may rely on your support in this truly national work in this neglected Public School". There is still no public swimming pool in East Balmain, the nearest being at Elkington Park.

Few Australians were enjoying themselves, but the people of Balmain were suffering more than most. Mary Quirk, Member for Balmain in the Legislative Assembly, wrote to Bob Heffron, Minister for Education in June 1944: "It is called the forgotten area". Baker wrote to the Department of Education the next month: "It appears that flats, factories and dwellings are of greater value to the nation than the general welfare of the children". The Valuer-General's Department admitted in October 1944, that the air-raid shelters diminished the play space available. The constant answer to demands that extra land be acquired was that the price was too high — yet delapidated homes were bought in East Balmain for as low as £150.

In any case, the department suggested the whole future of the school was in doubt. Inspector G.A. Morrow wrote in 1945 to the Director of Education, J.G. McKenzie:

"What might be considered in the future is the transfer of the primary pupils to Balmain school and the establishment at Nicholson Street of an Infants and Nursery School".

The post-war baby boom, immigration, and the replacement of old homes by blocks of flats was to give the school and the suburb a new lease of life, even if everyone didn't approve.

A boy of the 1930s *(Macleay Museum)*

Noel Arena with his mother, Josephine *(far left)* and with his sister, Florence

The Balmain tram on the corner of Darling and Nicholson Streets

Building the tram counterweight system down to Darling Street wharf *(all photos on this page from the Public Transport Commission)*

The Golden Cobb birdseed factory in Balmain, 1952 *(Macleay Museum)*

Opening of Housing Commission flats on the site of Durham House, Nicholson Street Balmain, 1949

9

"Living in the real world"

GETTING OUT AND MIXING IN

"Perhaps the judge could be forgiven for not knowing what the real world was like but anyone from Balmain will tell you that is an impossibility to live in such a community without occasionally coming into contact with people with criminal records." That is what Roger Degen, Member for Balmain in the Legislative Assembly, told the New South Wales Parliament in 1980.

Degen had been criticised in a report of the Woodward Royal Commission on Drug Trafficking, the judge accusing him of having "many unsavoury associates including a number of drug trafficking connections". Degen said in Parliament: "From his own private ivory tower on the North Shore, the judge may be able to be selective of the company he keeps, but any Member for Balmain who wants to hold his seat will be constantly seen in the pubs and clubs of his electorate". Although the Balmain branch of the Labor Party had passed a vote of no-confidence in their member, the parliamentary party rallied to his side. Rodney Cavalier, a member of the party's Left-wing, normally opposed to Right-wingers like Degen, said the only thing Degen was guilty of was "excessive loyalty" — to his friends, family and the Labor Party — and that he subscribed to the tradition "that you never scab on your mates". The Assembly voted on party lines to defeat a motion to have Degen expelled.

The opinions of both judge and politician shed some light on life in Balmain. Without doubt the judge was right to question the conduct of an elected Member of Parliament who drank "in public places with criminals", reported the *Sydney Morning Herald* on 15 August 1980. Yet Degen's riposte, that it was impossible to live in Balmain without coming into contact with criminals, also rang true, at least in 1980. Balmain and some of its identities were mentioned several times in the Woodward Royal Commission and the 1973–1974 Moffitt Royal Commission into organised crime in clubs. Yet, by 1983, many of these figures had moved from the area and there were signs that much of the organisation of crime had gone with them. By 1983 household theft was the main criminal activity in the suburb. The thieves were mostly unemployed youths.

Only a detailed study would show whether the people of Balmain were more — or less — law-abiding than the people of other Sydney suburbs. There is no doubt, however, that Balmain built up a reputation over the last hundred years as a "rough" suburb, a reputation that was only beginning to fade in the 1980s. The reputation itself is probably not as important as the effect it has on the people. Shady activities so well publicised through the Woodward Royal Commission did not stop affluent young people from moving to Balmain in the 1980s. Yet that "rough" reputation had led other people to move out.

A reporter wrote for the *Balmain Observer,* as early as 3 February 1886 that four young men charged with riotous behaviour in Weston Street were said to be "connected with the mob known as the 'Liver Push' (probably from Liverpool, England) and were decidedly notorious characters".

The newspaper in 1899 called attention to a gambling den in the upper part of a building known as the "Trades Hall".

> Now there are two of these schools in this suburb carrying on their gambling every night, not even Sunday night excepted, causing many young men to become enamoured with the spirit of gambling . . . The system employed is the tossing of coins . . . We are informed that the police know of the existence of these schools and prefer to allow them to go on as a preventative to the young men doing it on vacant lots and also for the reason that they know where to find any of their victims when the law requires them to face the magistrate.

In 1905, police swooped simultaneously on three betting shops, one known as the Lord Cardigan Divan. Police were swooping on gambling establishments before this time and have been ever since.

In 1935, Nicholson Street headmaster Charles Henry John Arter wrote to J.W. Hayes, Inspector of Schools at Rozelle, pointing out that youths were climbing on the school roof, after school hours, throwing stones, and making themselves "generally objectionable". He added: "There is also a report to the effect that they meet at the rear of the main building and play cards for money. I have communicated with Balmain police". More than 40 years later, a former Nicholson Street student was running one of Sydney's best-known illegal gambling casinos. In this sense, times hadn't changed much.

The "roughness" wasn't the only reason, of course, why some people left Balmain. Many young people simply grew up, married and moved to the northern beaches or to the outer western suburbs where there was more room. By the 1970s, some people were moving out because their job on the Balmain waterfront had gone, or because they couldn't afford to stay in a suburb which had become fashionable again.

Frank Martin stayed.

> There were plenty of stinks, fights, but that was part of your upbringing. There was a Stephens Street mob, a Pilcher's Paddock gang, the Rozelle mob and so on. The idea was to stick to your area. There was no housebreaking in those days. Some people say it was because there was a code of honour among the locals — they might rob a bank but they wouldn't knock off their neighbour's house. I think it was more a case of there being nothing to steal, only the ice chest. No one had any jewellery. And Balmain was a little village. Everyone knew one another and if you were caught doing something you shouldn't, you'd be ostracised. You'd pinch some paint from a local company, though, or some wire. That was part of the award. We used to have what we called the East End Yacht

Club, an excuse to gather over a barbecue and a few beers on Sunday mornings. You could always buy a shirt there, or a cheap pair of shoes.

> My brothers and sisters left the area. It was the ambition of the younger ones to move to Drummoyne, Gladesville or Ryde, to start a new life in a nice, new home. And Balmain had been a dirty place. The bedbugs could keep you awake at night, until we started using DDT. For every bag of copra brought in to Balmain on a boat, there were 5000 cockroaches. But we didn't mind this as kids. We were having too much fun. On my eleventh birthday we found what we thought were some firecrackers in an old engineering factory. We thought we'd have a practice for cracker night. But the crackers were distress rockets. It blew up the factory, lit up the whole East End and blew windows out of houses. My brother Henry — he was eight — had a fractured skull, perforated abdomen and intestines and lacerations. We were all pretty lucky.

Winifred Walker was a Miss Halliday, one of the engineering Hallidays of Balmain who made, among other things, all the school bells in New South Wales. Her mother, Alice Halliday, lived to be 102, never took any social security from the government and watched Balmain Rugby League team play until her final years, when she was visited regularly by such champions as Keith Barnes. Winifred, living at Bayview in 1983, didn't share Alice's passion for Balmain. Alice had a total of 13 children and 11 went to Nicholson Street. At one stage they lived in the rambling big house on the water that became famous as the site of the McGooley TV series of the 1960s. Mrs Walker said in 1983: "Nobody looked after their properties because nobody owned them. The place was very run down. Buckets of blood ran out of the hotels. The six o'clock swill was terrible". (Six o'clock hotel closing, introduced in 1916, continued in New South Wales until 1954. Men realising they had only an hour or so in the pub after work would drink so quickly that street drunkenness was much more prevalent.) Mrs Walker continued:

> The Volunteer in Darling Street was called the Blood and Guts. People would say, "It's six o'clock, let's go and see the fights" — not even "Let's go and see if there are any fights". I had two sons who went to Nicholson Street and they loved Balmain. But we could see it wasn't the right place to bring kids up. When we moved the kids resented it at first.

Mrs Dolly Anderson who has stayed, said: "In the early days Balmain was aristocracy, all the ship's captains. Somebody got married from the big house across the road from Saint Mary's. She walked across the road on a red carpet. But Balmain was slummy in our day. People used to say, 'Where do you live?' . . . 'Balmain' . . . 'Oooh, Balmain?'".

Marcia Britton stayed, too. She thought: "The only homes looked after in the Depression were those owned by the people who lived in them. Most people rented. If you owned a house, then you were really big time, like the Braids . . . 'Oooh you're going out with a Braid,' they'd say".

Connie Blunden was a Braid until she married Frank Blunden, whose father had come from England to help build the Bridge. Frank and Connie both stayed. "I think it's a marvellous place," said Frank, "always has been. You get to know everybody".

Ivy Blunden pawned the family sheets during the Depression, married Stan Edwards, moved out of Balmain and came back. Stan owned several businesses before moving into the Commercial Hotel in 1956. It was the year television — black and white — was introduced in Australia and the pub raised £700 to provide a TV set for the school. Ivy hadn't wanted to go into the pub. "I cried for a fortnight". But Ivy and Stan could see the possibilities.

> We used to have 280 customers at lunchtime, mainly from the Adelaide company. I hated some parts of pub life, though. I wasn't popular with the women of Balmain. They used to say I was keeping their men out drinking. There were a lot of drunks around during the six o'clock swill. And some women used to come up and do their vegetables in the ladies' parlour, a dirty old room where drinks were passed through a window. I remember the old men too, playing dominoes. I wouldn't serve them until they'd gone out to have a meal. I'd worry they would fall over. The women wouldn't talk to me because they blamed me for leading their men to drink. I'd tell them the men would drink anyhow. We laugh about it now. We all talk to one another. I'm happy here.

Roderick West, principal of Trinity Grammar School in 1983, was born in 1933 in the McGooley house where the Hallidays once lived:

> I remember walking up the hill and being pursued by enormous dogs that seemed to be waiting in their lairs to spring out at me. That fear of dogs has lasted until this day. My father (Harry West, the sailmaker) was born in Balmain, the youngest of 11 kids and was very much a Balmain kid, a craftsman, sewing with his hands. His philosophy was that you get out of school as soon as possible and earn a living. I had to stand up and fight my father, who counted on my becoming an accountant and joining the family company. My mother was a bit of a blue stocking who was determined to get out of Balmain as soon as she could. One reason was White's dockyard across from our house. My mother thought the language of the men too blue for us. So we moved to Hunters Hill. My parents thought the people there a bit snooty, so we moved to Drummoyne.

Roderick West's sister, now Mrs Catherine Hawkshaw, said:

> Our social life centred on the church — lovely fetes, socials, plays and so on. I remember the Sunday school picnics at Clifton Gardens in a new frock and new sandshoes. But I had my mouth washed out with soap when I was two years old for saying "bloody". After leaving Balmain I always had a dread of having to go back there to live. I disliked the dirt. It was pretty squalid.

John Shackcloth's reasons for leaving were much the same. He had come to Balmain from Scotland in 1924 and recalled his first day at school:

> At recess I saw something crawling up an office window — it was a lizard, I'd

never seen one before. I threw a pebble at it gently. Then I felt my ear taken firmly between a thumb and forefinger. It was the teacher. I was trembling like five leaves. In those days Balmain was not very hygienic. Our little place just about broke my mother's heart. People don't like to talk about it, but the terraces were riddled with lice. I remember my mother treating the beds with caustic soda and hot water in the back yard. It was a problem to keep vermin out; there were cockroaches galore. We were happy to get away, though most people seemed happy there. Despite everything, it seemed a healthy place. They bred them tough in those days.

Jack Morgan, who went to school at Nicholson Street and became the East End chemist, said: "To be an East Ender you had to have had a couple of generations there. Everyone else was a foreigner". His mother was a schoolteacher and felt herself part of the old social order — above the ruck in Balmain, but below certain citizens. The Morgans had a tennis court at their Darling Street home. "But most people came from large working class families," said Jack Morgan. "Today the families are smaller and half the couples aren't married at all".

Bill Brunton, aged 84 in 1983, recalled the "roughness" of Balmain, although it had never been rough enough for him to move to another suburb. One gang would meet another and the conversation would go something like this: "Hello, how long since we had a fight?"

"Okay, let's get a mob together".

"Right, we went to your place last time. Come down to us".

Brunton said his sister even arranged fights in a paddock in Church Street. And he recalled political candidates under pressure at Balmain Town Hall.

Candidate:
Ladies and gentlemen . . . (candidate hit with bag of flour. He dusts himself off).
Candidate:
Ladies and gentlemen . . . (candidate, hit with tomato, ends his attempt to speak).

Some of the Weldons have stayed, but most have gone, mainly to the north shore. Sid Weldon and his wife Hazel lived in 1983 in a block of home units looking across to Goat Island and up the harbour to the Bridge. Goat Island was first occupied as an ammunition and gunpowder store built by convicts. One convict was Charles "Bony" Anderson, who, according to legend, was chained to a rock for looking at passing ships instead of working. He is said to have hollowed out an alcove in the sandstone, making what is now known as Anderson's Couch. When the convicts were moved from Goat Island to Cockatoo Island in 1838, British troops guarded the ammunition. In 1900 it was used as a bacteriological station to fight the bubonic plague then raging in Sydney. In 1983 the island was run by the Maritime Services Board, but several proposals have been suggested for it. They include that it be made a central part of another harbour bridge, that it be the site for a casino, or even a heliport.

Sid Weldon's grandfather, from the north of Ireland, was in charge of the ammunitions store on the island way back in the 1860s, winning a service medal from Queen Victoria for his efforts. Sid's father Vivian, known as Dick, was one of 13 Weldon children born on Goat Island and became skipper of the showboat *Kalang*. Sid didn't like the sea so much, but loved mucking about in tugs. He was still mucking about in tugs in 1983, aged 77. Hazel's father, Captain H. Tanglin, helped save seven men from the *Oakland,* which sank off Port Stephens in 1903 with the loss of 11 men.

When Sid and Hazel Weldon's view down the harbour was partly blocked by home units, they agreed: ''If you can't beat them, join them''. They bought a unit, intending to stay there until they were carried out.

Janice Davis is a Weldon who married and moved to Beacon Hill. ''Balmain used not to be a fashionable place, but people always said 'hello' to one another. The mothers used to be out the front of the house a lot, chatting over the fence and sweeping up. It was a close-knit community — it's not so close over here. Yet most of the young people used to move out when they married, trying to do something better with their lives''.

Pam Saunders, another Weldon, married and won a Crown Land ballot at Berowra. ''We weren't in a hurry to get out, but that's what most people seemed to be doing then [1968]''.

Eunice Hemsley, *née* Weldon, lived in 1983 in a home unit overlooking the school she attended 60 years ago. ''My two children just got married and looked around for a home. But I would die if I had to leave''.

Donald McPherson hasn't left, either. He was one of 10 children born to Emily Florence McPherson. (Another was Leonard, who became known as the ''Mr Big'' of Sydney crime, a description he resolutely denied in 1968. He told the Moffitt Royal Commission that his basic income — $40 — came from managing a motel in Birchgrove. Asked to explain his relatively affluent lifestyle, he said: ''I do the best I can''.) Don McPherson, born in 1906, told in 1983 how a child had once wandered off the street and been taken in by a Balmain family. ''No one seemed to know where he came from, but they took him in and sent him to Nicholson Street. That sort of thing wasn't surprising in Balmain. He joined up in World War II and was one of the first killed. His parents probably never knew''.

Defending, in the New South Wales Parliament in 1978, his administration's efforts against organised crime, ex-Balmain boy Neville Wran named another Balmain boy, Stanley John Smith, as a leading figure in the Sydney underworld. Smith, sometimes known as Stan the Man, had been barred from entering Hong Kong with Leonard McPherson in 1966. Asked to explain his income to the Woodward Royal Commission, particularly how he managed to bank $34 000 in 18 months — twice his yearly income from his job as supervisor with the Balmain Welding Company — Smith said he regularly won money gambling.

Some years ago Billo Robinson, ex-Nicholson Street School, helped a little old lady across the street with her parcels, not knowing who she was. Stan the Man approached Billo later: ''I've heard reports that you helped my mother across the road . . .'' ''Cut the bullshit,'' said Billo. Balmain can be like that.

4th, 5th and 6th classes, 1948

3rd and 4th classes, 1950

1A and 2nd class, 1953

Year of the crew-cut, 1959

5th and 6th classes, 1962

Rugby League team, 1966

Informality inside the school, 1982

Adventure playground, 1982

10

"The kids threw away their crusts"

REACHING A CENTURY

The Stannards have been associated with Balmain for as long as most people remember. Bruce Stannard, a writer and TV producer who won a Niemen Fellowship to Harvard University in 1982, attended Nicholson Street School from 1951. He tells how it used to be:

> This is one of Australia's busiest industrial areas. There are dozens of ships at the big repair yards and engineering works strung out right around the waterfront. The incessant hammering and banging of rivets is everywhere, like the drumming of summer cicadas. The air is heavy with factory smoke. Grey plumes waft from terrace chimney pots, too; a lot of Balmain people still cook on fuel stoves.
>
> The seven o'clock siren has just signalled the change of shift and the boilermakers, ironworkers and the ship painters and dockers mill about. The streets are full of men in dark blue dungarees and grey Akubra hats. The factory women are in uniform, too, their hair tied up in scarves. People queue at the tram stops along Darling Street. In Nicholson Street, the men swarm out of the big Adelaide Steamship Company yard and walk like troops in line abreast, up the street to the tram, down to the ferry or, simply home. For most of the men live here, in the little terrace houses and weatherboard bungalows, close to their work. Even at seven in the morning there are a dozen or so kids in the school playground. Their mothers work at the Palmolive and Unilever factories and they come to school when mum leaves home for the morning shift. At the bottom of the playground lies the forbidden world of The Jungle, a thicket of thorns, a dark, mysterious place where only the Big Kids dare go. The Jungle is where the Big Kids smoke Greys, Craven A and Capstan. It's where the Secret Society meets. It's where the Gang performs its initiation rights. It's where you learn the swear words that earn a thrashing, sometimes with a feather duster, at home. The Jungle looks impenetrable. In fact, it is honeycombed with an intricate tunnel system. Intrepid 10 year olds have burrowed through the brambles to create their own cool, green hideaway, utterly cut off from teachers, parents and anyone else on the outside. This is Nicholson Street's Middle Earth. The teachers say no one is allowed in The Jungle. The Big Kids go nonetheless.
>
> Girls are excluded, of course. In fact, throughout the school, there is virtually no contact between girls and boys. Sometimes boys are forced to touch girls during "awful sissy stuff" like folk dancing, but generally the boys think girls

are to be avoided like the plague. And the feeling is mutual. The girls are kept pretty much to the top playground, just behind the school building, which is mostly loose gravel and marked with dangerous pot holes. The gravel gouges bloody holes in kneecaps. All self-respecting boys have at least one scarred or lacerated kneecap or shin.

The Big Kids play footie, cricket and marbles on The Bottom, an area of sloping, tussocky grass running down from the toilet blocks. The marbles ring is drawn in dirt with a stick. Kids have their marbles in calico sacks, swapping their prized Connie Agates for Cats Eyes. The little kids tend to hang around the fringes.

The toilet blocks are antiquated, cream-painted wooden buildings that are always hosed out in the mornings and reek of brown phenol disinfectant. The school is heated by open fires and there's a wood and coal storage area at the back of the boy's lavatory, usually called "the dunny". Above the boys' urinal is a trapdoor. Grab the urinal pipe and swing up — keeping telltale footprints off the wall, and you enter one of the Secret Society's hideouts. In the gloom there are candles, matches, comics, cigarettes and lots of dust. It's here that blood brothers are made by cutting fingers with razor blades and pressing the bloody parts together. It was an old Apache ceremony Randolph Scott showed us one Saturday afternoon at the Hoyts.

About 200 kids mill about the top playground when the assembly bell sounds. The huge old brass bell is swung by a rope from the top of an ancient hardwood post near the flagpole. The headmaster, short and scowling in a three-piece tweed suit, climbs three steps to the top of a podium to survey lines being straightened by fussing teachers. There's the tall and sometimes rather fierce Miss Bruce, the middle-aged, portly and silver-haired Mr Ross and the angelic Miss Archer. The boys have secret crushes on the lovely Miss Archer. She disappoints everyone later by going off to marry a complete stranger.

The headmaster booms: "Good morning, boys and girls". "Good morning headmaster," they chorus with absolute obedience. Two boys haul the Australian flag all the way to the top of the whitewashed pole and the headmaster doesn't have to tell the children what comes next. He simply counts — 'One, two, three' and they launch into a rousing version of *God Save the King*. The King is seen as an important figure in the school. The Queen will be too, when she succeeds to the throne in 1952. There are few notions of an Australian republic. Royal portraits decorate every classroom.

The classrooms are large and cold; the floors are bare. Desks are ornate cast iron and dark hardwood with twin porcelain inkwells. The children use wooden pens with nibs and teachers demand that the writing remains in the Victorian copperplate style.

At 10.45 we watch as the milk truck rumbles down the street, with a great clinking of bottles. The "milk boys" — it is a great lurk for missing at least 15 minutes of class — dash out and leap up on the truck. Milk is held to be an essential part of every schoolchild's diet. They enjoy it at playlunch. Teachers even use it as a bribe, "Sit up straight and don't make a sound and I'll give you an extra bottle of milk".

At lunchtime most children eat only the middle out of their sandwiches. Crusts are usually tossed into bins. The school day ends as it began, with the sound of the bell. After the kids have gone, the sirens sound again around the waterfront. The shifts change; the streets are full of men in blue again.

So the kids threw away their crusts. In so doing, they horrified their frugal parents who had known the Depression, but their action reflected a new optimism that had taken seed across the land. Australians had to look back to the years before World War I to recall the golden days, days when they were untroubled by recession or war. Now the golden days were back. Wool sold for a pound a pound and graziers danced on tables at the Australia Hotel. The Snowy Mountains scheme was built. Migrants boosted the work-force. Social welfare was improved. Sure, there was some inflation and the Korean war brought fear of a nuclear holocaust but this counted for little when everyone who wanted to work could get a job, when children leaving school could pick and choose their employer. Sure, with hindsight the fifties were a little dull, culture was at a low ebb, the migrants hadn't had time to enrich the society, politics were bland and lacking in original thought. But that counted for little when workers had the 40-hour week from 1948, with two full days off a week and plenty of overtime if they wished.

Balmain, though, had its problems. Mary Quirk, the Member for Balmain in the Legislative Assembly, wrote to the Minister for Education, Clive Evatt, in 1949 of the "many complaints about undesirable persons loitering in the porch at Nicholson Street. There is a great need for a pair of high gates. Drinking, language and wrongdoing goes on all hours of the night. I promised the P and C, also members of the Balmain ALP that it would be attended to at once".

The migrants and the baby boom made it essential that new homes were built. New South Wales authorities had submitted to federal officials in 1943 that 14.5 per cent of Sydney's dwellings were substandard and that more than 67 000 additional dwellings would be needed to house the city's population of one and a half million.

In 1948 the Report on the Planning Scheme, carried out by the Cumberland County Council, delineated the degree of sub-standard housing in Sydney. More than half the houses of Balmain were included, with parts of East Balmain thought to be in the worst condition. The New South Wales Housing Commission moved into Balmain, building flats but neglecting to provide open playing areas — a neglect that had begun with the original land grants in the area.

In education, there was now a chance to introduce the progressive ideas that had been delayed by war. Equal pay was granted to women teachers in 1958.

However, there was a shortage of teachers: their number rose from 11 000 in 1945 to nearly 27 000 20 years later and to 46 000 in the late 1970s. But the Australian Council for Educational Research reported in 1953 that the "necessity to secure more teachers by all possible means has distracted too much of the attention of parliamentary, administrative and professional association leaders from the more fundamental purpose of the education system''.

According to Gordon Greenwood, author of the book entitled *Australia,* the education system has nearly always reflected the preoccupation with providing near equal opportunity for all. Education was seen as a democratic weapon for the ending of class distinction. The renewal in the 1970s of the debate over state aid to private schools brought the equal-opportunity argument back to centre stage. One side to the argument is that equal opportunity is central to Australian democracy; the other is that such a preoccupation has sacrificed the talents of the few to the needs of the many. Even Henry Lawson, that hero of the workers, put this argument:

There'll be higher education
for the toilin', starvin' clown.
And the rich an' educated
shall be educated down.

As Australia boomed through the fifties and into the sixties, the toilin' children of Nicholson Street continued to labour under difficulties. There was not much equal opportunity in this part of the world, although many children were to rise above it.

Change was on the way. Teachers and parents were more politically aware and more militant. Gough Whitlam's Labor Party wasn't far off winning the 1969 federal election, with a program including increased funds for education. It was also an age when authority was being questioned. The Vietnam war saw to that, with the help of colour television. Viewers saw the war — live and dead — in their living rooms and their questioning of the authorities who conducted that war finally brought it to an end.

At Nicholson Street, authority was being questioned, too. In the 1920s there had been a prolonged argument over whether schoolchildren should salute the flag. The Education Minister insisted they should, every Monday morning . . .

I honour my God,
I serve my King,
I salute my flag.

The argument surfaced again in 1954, when schools were instructed to fly the flag on the first day of every week of term and to recognise it in a fitting manner . . .

I honour my God,
I serve my Queen,
I salute my flag.

At Nicholson Street in the 1960s a parent ordered her child not to stand for the national anthem. Yet more fundamental protests were coming. Gough Whitlam's commitment to education on the grounds that the future of the nation lay with the minds of the children was shared by most young parents in Balmain. Their expectations of the education system had been raised. Yet, when Niels Warren became president of the Nicholson Street P and C Association in 1973, ''. . . there were hardly any books in the library''. Warren said: ''It was a poor little underprivileged school''. Children had been leaving the school because their parents thought it less than adequate. Enrolments dipped to 78 in the 1960s, putting the whole future of the school at risk.

Led by Warren and articulate parents adept at the politics of education, like Frances Milne, they put pressure on the headmaster. They wanted their children to attend a good local school rather than have to travel or to go to a private school. They put pressure on the Education Department. ''As far as we were concerned,'' said Warren, ''it was the headmaster or our kids. And we decided, quite cold-bloodedly, that our kids would win''. The principal and another teacher were forced out at the end of the year, presumably to work out their careers at schools where the P and C was weaker or non-existent.

Radicalism took other forms. The Education Department wanted to demolish a cottage in the school grounds but the parents wanted it kept for after-school activities. They co-opted Jack Mundey, leader of the Builders Labourers' Federation and architect of the Green Bans movement so effective in Sydney at the time. A green ban was placed on the cottage and parents slept there overnight in order to deter any demolition team that might move in at dawn. The parents lost the battle for the cottage but secured funds for an after-school centre in the main building. Another cottage in the grounds was saved and was still being used as part of the school in 1983, by which time Lyn Thomson had become the school's first woman principal.

Another former Nicholson Street student had become Balmain's latest sporting hero. Wayne Pearce went to Nicholson Street in the 1960s and to Britain in 1982 with the unbeaten Australian Rugby League team. He was named ''man of the tour'' by his colleagues. Old hands in the suburb were talking about him in the same breath as Chook Fraser and Archie Jackson and Dawn Fraser. Dawn Fraser grew up in Birchgrove and was first coached by her cousin Ray Miranda, an East Ender. ''He showed me the rudiments of using my arms and legs in the water and first made me enthusiastic about racing. I'd won my first race at eight, in a 33⅓ yards [30.5 metres] tiny tot championship — using a little dog paddle, a little sidestroke with a trudgeon kick, and a little overarm''. Dawn Fraser became arguably the greatest swimmer of all time. She was still manager of the Riverview Hotel, Birchgrove, in 1983.

One sadness about the period was that some older residents, unable to compete with the young affluent, were moving out. On the other hand, people connected with the arts and the universities were adding new dimensions to the suburb. These included Frank Moorhouse, David Williamson, Nathan Waks, Judy Morris, John Gaden, Charles Colman and Peter Carey. In an article for *Le Monde,* Frances Kelly wrote about ''Le Ghetto de Balmain''. Moorhouse, in *Days of Wine and Rage* pointed out that, for the Balmain economy, literary grants were the equivalent of a new factory opening.

The suburb became the target for jokes and satire, especially as the Whitlam years turned sour with the approach of another international recession. Moorhouse wrote in an article in the *Bulletin* published on 30 August 1975:

The hostility was not really against the physical suburb of Balmain (usually

> extended in journalistic commentary to include Carlton in Melbourne and sometimes the whole of Adelaide). Balmain became short-hand for the fantasised (and sometimes real) way of life of some of the people of Balmain, Carlton and Adelaide. It was hostility against the new writing, especially young writing, sexual explicitness, experiment.

As Moorhouse pointed out, Balmain made other things beside poetry, lesbians and revolution. It made Pears soap in the Unilever factory. He noted the irony that Balmain made the most middle-class of soaps. In 1982 he might have noted another irony — the Town Hall Hotel, which had been a blood house in years past and later was managed by a footballer, was taken over by a happy band of homosexuals who transformed it into the most attractive pub it had ever been.

As for revolution, it never quite made it in Balmain. Even in Kerr's coup of 1975, anger over Whitlam's dismissal simmered rather than boiled over. The people of Fitzroy, Melbourne, were more radical than those of Balmain during the Depression, actually trading blows with police over evicted neighbours. In 1975 too, there was more radicalism in other places. Graham Phair, a Youth and Community Services officer, spoke a common sentiment: "They can take government away from us but they can't take Balmain away. Let's go to the pub".

Inspector George Stone, of the New South Wales Police Force, said: "There are only two kinds of people in the world — those who live in Balmain and those who wish they did".

Joe Wran was philosophical about the changes in the suburb. He admired the way in which many of the old houses had been restored. But he thought they must be filled with couples without children who ate take-away food and with large dogs who fouled the footpaths.

Writer Ruth Park described it as a "rare, felicitous place" and quoted a local: "Yeah, one of these days Balmain may join the Commonwealth. But I dunno. We're still chewing over whether we'll join New South".

Heather Jacobs, who was Heather Smith when she went to Nicholson Street, recalled: "It was real macho for boys to find something with wheels and go straight down hills, over the wharf and into the water". In 1983 she was worried about development in Balmain. "I'm talking about an emotional issue. I feel invaded and it's just wrong". She thought the years 1950 to 1965 were the golden years:

> Our fathers worked here because we lived here. Now they have to go to work at Blacktown or Botany and people who work in town can afford to live here. A woman who lives next to me is a solicitor. She was telling me over the fence, "Oh, Balmain must have been a dreary little place", which made my hackles rise.
>
> I said, "Oh, I suppose it was. But there was more happiness here than anywhere".
>
> "Oh, do you know the place?"
>
> "Yes, I was born here".
>
> She was very apologetic.

Carol Flecknoe, *née* Smith, said: "There's certainly a more friendly attitude here than in other trendy suburbs. You have to accept people. New people have to assimilate with the old".

Diane Stewart, part of the second of three generations of the one family to attend Nicholson Street, said:

> Generations of families were born and bred here until the last 20 years, when we began to get blow-ins, hippies, when it became fashionable. I can go to mum's up the coast and say "hello" to all the people I used to say "hello" to in Balmain. People would dearly love to buy here and can't, with the inflation and the blow-ins and the professionals who want to live close to the city and use the ferry. They have the dollars. If I move there'll be no more Balmain for the family and there's no way you could get back once you've left.

Nicholson Street was classified as a "disadvantaged school" in 1974, as part of one of the great reforms in education — to spend money where it was most needed. Ancillary staff allowed more individual attention for pupils; the library, which had been housed in a cupboard, was given a whole room; the after-school centre blossomed; the rigidity of the old desk system was broken down. The school looked brighter and friendlier; the learning process became more flexible. With the economic recession of the 1980s, funds were drying up and Balmain was quite clearly less disadvantaged than some other areas of Sydney.

There were signs of economic recovery late in 1983 but a typical concern of Australians was still how to get — or keep — their jobs. It remained to be seen what effect this would have on the young children at primary schools throughout Australia.

Margaret West outside Nicholson Street School, 1935

Acknowledgments

JOURNALS AND NEWSPAPERS

Some writers for journals and newspapers have been cited as sources of information and others were consulted. In acknowledgment, the names of the publications and authors are as follows:

Leichhardt Historical Journal. Nadia Wheatley, “Responses of the Balmain People to the Depression”. No. 1; Peter Reynolds, “Goat and Cockatoo: Two Islands off Balmain”. No. 9; John Flower, “James McDonald, Architect of Balmain”. No. 8.

Standard Weekly, Sun, Sydney Morning Herald, Sydney Mail, Balmain Observer, Freeman's Journal, Argus, Bulletin, Sunday Mail and Sunday Telegraph.

Cumberland County Council, Report on the Planning Scheme, 1948; Australian National Opinion Polls, *Sydney Morning Herald,* 1978.

UNPUBLISHED MANUSCRIPTS

Unpublished manuscripts have been referred to as source material, and where possible their title is acknowledged with the author:

Lady Storey, untitled manuscript. Barbara Foy, *Kid Sister.* S.N. Hogg, *Balmain Past and Present.* Family papers held by Keith Storey.

BOOKS

Authors and titles of published books relevant to the story of Balmain:
H.V. Evatt, *Australian Labor Leader*. Peter Reynolds and Paul Flottmann, *Half a Thousand Acres.* C.M.H. Clark, *A History of Australia.* Vol. 4. Ruth Park, *The Companion Guide to Sydney.* Humphrey McQueen, *Social Sketches of Australia 1888 – 1975.* John Kerr, *Matters for Judgment.* W. Farmer Whyte, *W.M. Hughes, His Life and Times.* Donald Horne, *In Search of Billy Hughes.* L.F. Fitzhardinge, *That Fiery Particle.* Reginald Thornton and A.W. Sommerville, *Balmain Retrospect.* Ernst Jünger Werke, *Lagebücher.* John Wright, *Saint John's Church Balmain.* John Barrett, *Falling In: Australians and "Boy Conscription" 1911 – 1915.* Barbara Whitley (ed.), *The Chronicles of Suzy Em.* A.G. Moyes, *A Century of Cricketers.* P.R. Stephensen, *The History and Description of Sydney Harbour.* Wendy Lowenstein, *Weevils in the Flour.* Bruce Stannard, *Blue-water Bushmen.* Jill Roe (ed.), *Twentieth Century Sydney.* Gordon Greenwood, *Australia.* Harry Gordon, *Dawn Fraser*. Frank Moorhouse, *Days of Wine and Rage.*

OTHER REFERENCES

Sydney and the Bush, a Pictorial History of Education in New South Wales, a publication to commemorate the centenary of the Department of Education of New South Wales. Education Department Archives. *Dictionary of Australian Biography.* Vol. 2. Commonwealth of Australia Census, 1933. *The Australian Encyclopaedia.* Vol. 1.